Paul Clayton

Paul Clayton made his debut as an actor in infant school at the age of seven and from that moment on knew what he wanted to be. A prominent member of the National Youth Theatre throughout the mid-seventies, he trained at Manchester Polytechnic School of Theatre and made his professional debut on stage at the Royal Exchange Theatre, Manchester, in 1978. As an actor and a director he has worked in York, Nottingham, Leicester, Exeter, Birmingham, Colchester, Chichester, Watford, Newbury, Cambridge and Greenwich. He spent three-and-a-half years with the Royal Shakespeare Company during the 1980s, and West End work includes *Romeo and Juliet* and *Scissor Happy*, an improvised whodunnit with The Comedy Store Players at the Duchess Theatre.

Paul is probably best-known for his television appearances, which include five series of the award-winning sitcom *Peep Show*, and two series of the BAFTA-winning *Him & Her*. He has played regular characters in *Coronation Street*, *Doctors* and *Hollyoaks*, as well as making appearances in *Doctor Who*, *My Family*, *One Foot in the Grave*, *Drop the Dead Donkey*, *55° North*, *Wire in the Blood*, *Vera*, *The Secret of Crickley Hall*, *Law and Order UK*, *Hotel Babylon*, *He Kills Coppers*, *The Frankenstein Chronicles*, *Mr Selfridge*, and *Wolf Hall*. Film work includes *Ali G In Da House*, *Fakers*, *The Man Who Cried*, *Gambit* and *The Rise*.

Paul specialises in working in the corporate sector around his film and television commitments, working in role-play and coaching senior executives one-to-one. He has staged over 350 large-scale corporate events across the world and his book, *So You Want to Be a Corporate Actor?*, also published by Nick Hern Books, is a comprehensive guide for actors and directors wanting to work in this sector.

He is a regular columnist for *The Stage* and an approved blogger for *The Huffington Post*. He is currently Chairman of the Board of the Actors Centre in Covent Garden, and a patron of the children's charity Grimm & Co, based in his hometown of Rotherham.

THE
WORKING
ACTOR

THE ESSENTIAL GUIDE
TO A SUCCESSFUL CAREER

PAUL CLAYTON

NICK HERN BOOKS
London
www.nickhernbooks.co.uk

A Nick Hern Book

The Working Actor
first published in Great Britain in 2016
by Nick Hern Books Limited, The Glasshouse,
49a Goldhawk Road, London W12 8QP

Cover design: Christopher Clegg

Designed and typeset by Nick Hern Books
Printed and bound in Great Britain by
Ashford Colour Press, Gosport, Hampshire

A CIP catalogue record for this book is available
from the British Library

ISBN 978 1 84842 436 4

For Elliot, Adam and Luke
who have so much ahead

Contents

Acknowledgements

A great deal of this book is based on personal opinion, but it has been a joy during the writing of it to talk to so many people and find out their thoughts. Thanks to everyone I interviewed, including Hannah Miller, Catherine Willis, Louise Grainger, Pippa Harrison, Will Wollen, Grant Attwell, Abigail Longstaff, Mariel Whitmond, Marysia Trembecka, Malcolm Browning, Richard Holborn, the Actors Centre, The Actors' Guild, and Alan Lean.

And thanks to my friends and colleagues who feature in the book and feature prominently in my life as a Working Actor: my corporate colleague Marianne O'Connor; respected friends Nick Dunning and Sarah Berger; my fantastic agent Amanda Howard and all the staff at AHA Talent, including my voice-over agent Laura Milne; my accountant Tim Haggard; my brilliant editor Matt Applewhite, and all the staff at Nick Hern Books who make it all a delight; and last but not least, my partner Richard Howle, who copes brilliantly with it all.

Introduction

In my role as Chairman of the Board of the Actors Centre, I've hosted a series of lunchtime interviews with actors at various stages of their careers, helping them share their experience and expertise with others. Partly out of laziness, and partly out of a desire to achieve some sort of commonality in the framework for the interviews, I begin each one with the question: 'How did it all start? When was that moment that you knew that this was what you wanted to do?' The answers proved revealing. For Juliet Stevenson, it was reading a poem at school. For Josie Lawrence, it was finding out that she could entertain members of her family. For Douglas Hodge, it was a natural step from being a teenage impressionist. Mark Rylance recalled helping to build the scenery for a high-school play in America. Sir Derek Jacobi remembered a particular feeling as he ran down the street wearing his mother's wedding veil.

For all of the interviewees, however, one thing was the same. There had been one moment when they knew the only thing they wanted to be was an actor. I think my own particular Damascene conversion happened in Miss Woodcock's class, late on a Thursday afternoon, in an infant school nestling in the foothills and slag heaps of the Soviet Socialist Republic of South Yorkshire. Having press-ganged Susan Clarke and Christine Evans into sharing the stage with me, I played the role of a heroic soldier battling for his loved one against the forces of an evil witch. Imaginatively titled *Evil Spirits*, and with its envelope-pushing casting of myself as the heroic, and no doubt heterosexual, soldier, it entertained the other members of our class for nearly ten minutes. I remember the applause, and I remember thinking: 'I like this.' From that moment on, I can honestly say that I knew what I wanted to be. An actor. I was seven.

Getting there, doing it, and making a living out of it, is what this book is about. I've managed to do that now for nearly forty years, something of which I am proud. I've spent a great deal of time unemployed. There have been weeks when seven imaginative ways with a baked potato has been my diet. Approaching sixty, I'd like to think I can call myself 'a Working Actor'. It says 'actor' on my passport, and it says 'actor' on my tax return. I make a living out of it, and I know that I'm incredibly lucky to have a job that I always wanted and that I still enjoy.

Luck is obviously a great part of success, and that has to be acknowledged. Luck can be helped along, though, and working hard at your career will bring its own rewards. Understanding the business, how it works, and your place in it, is crucial. How to look at the work that is out there, the jobs, the opportunities, and how to talk to people who have the power to give you those jobs, and to give you those opportunities. To find out how they make their choices. To find out what you can do to maximise the chance of their choice being *you*. That's what this book aims to do. To help you manage your day-to-day life as an actor. No one can teach you to act, but you can learn how to be an actor. A Working Actor. This book looks at ideas for the Working Actor of all ages.

One of the most important pieces of advice I think I've ever been given was from a fabulous old tutor called John McGregor at my drama school. He'd been a young hopeful at the RSC in the mid-fifties, alongside Olivier and Ian Holm. It hadn't worked for John in terms of stardom, but it had worked for him in terms of being a Working Actor. When he was our technique tutor at Manchester Polytechnic in the mid-seventies, he was still regularly appearing in television dramas and making a good living out of his acting. His mantra was one I have tried to follow ever since:

'Every day do at least one thing that might lead to work, and then get on with living your life.'

I think what he was trying to say was don't let the whole of your life be consumed by being an out-of-work actor. Don't forget to be a person. People buy people. So often in audition situations, sitting on the other side of the table, I have seen people come in absolutely desperate for the job to the point where I have had no chance to get to know them as a person. As a result, there is no hook with which I have been able to engage with them. They haven't got the job.

This book consists of twenty-six subjects. An eclectic mix, and made as a result of my own individual choice. At the end of each article is a work task. So, on the basis of Mr McGregor's mantra, this book gives you at least five weeks of one thing to do each day before getting on with your life. Assuming you take the weekend off! Not all of them may apply to all of you, but if just one of them leads to something, then I have done my job.

There may be a lucky few who, after leaving drama school, will jump from job to job, but for the vast majority it will be a constant fight, a struggle, to keep that employment as continuous as possible. It will require huge reserves of energy and focus to cope with unemployment, and it will rely on a constant input of imagination and creativity to maximise the opportunities that come along.

Not for nothing do people call it 'The Industry' or 'The Business' – a business is exactly what it is, and that's how you have to treat it and behave in it if you are to succeed.

I sincerely hope that this book helps. Helps you on a day-to-day basis. Helps you to manage your career as a business, and to maximise your potential. Above all, I hope it helps you realise those childhood dreams.

1. Getting started

'I want to be an actor.'

From the moment I started saying that, aged seven, it was all I wanted to be. It came as a great surprise when I went to drama school to discover there were some people who hadn't made this decision until much later in life. I thought it was a childhood dream for all concerned. Something that, once you got it into your brain, that was it. Think back to the moment when it happened for you. What made you take that decision to be an actor? What was the initial spur? One thing seems clear: once that thought is in place, it's very hard to ignore it. It's been said that you don't choose to be an actor; it chooses you. Something has been set in motion that is going to govern your life for many years to come. For just how long will depend on how well you manage to make it work.

Let me be upfront about it: this book can't get you work. If there were some magic formula to getting a job, I would publish it, everybody would buy it, and I would now be languishing on a sunbed somewhere in the Southern Hemisphere. There is no easy answer. Just how do you make that jump from training into the world of work? What you need to tap into is the wealth of experience and guidance that can be brought together and given to you for assimilation, and for you to use for your benefit. Not working can be very hard. Your contact with other actors can be minimal. You don't feel as though you're in the swing of things, and that feeling is not very conducive to getting work. Chatting with other actors, you learn what is going on, and how you might use the information to the best effect. Much of the success in getting jobs is having the right information. You need good solid information from people in the know. Working Actors, agents, casting directors, producers, and directors. Tapping into the opinions and guidance of people with experience is an exceptionally valuable way of increasing your potential.

Getting started for many people can be a great struggle. These days when that flame of thespian desire is lit, it's great to be able to go online and find out information as to how to proceed. Information on all possible training routes is just a mouse-click away. Way back in the days of my youth, when men still walked the streets with red flags in front of cars, and a cheery gas lighter carried his flame from lamp to lamp each smog-ridden dusk, it was harder to find out just how the world of show business linked to South Yorkshire. But link it I did. The National Youth Theatre was my first step, an organisation that still provides a platform for many young people to start their journey today. It was as part of the company in the early seventies that I suddenly realised that drama school was a possibility, even for someone like me from a background and place from which actors just didn't seem to come. If no one in your family has ever ventured into this world before, it's easy to question whether you have any right to be there. The answer is that you do. If you have a passion to do something, then that passion can carry you a long way. So often in social situations, on holiday, or in casual conversation, when it's revealed that I am an actor, there is a response from someone in the group: 'Ah yes. I wanted to be an actor. I used to do it a lot when I was young. But I decided I wanted a proper job. With a salary.'

On hearing this, or any one of its hundred variations, I nod, smile and say: 'Well, it can be difficult.' Inwardly my thoughts are less kind. I'm thinking: 'Actually, you didn't want to be an actor. Because once you do, certainly in the beginning, you cease to make rational decisions such as "I want a salary." You want to be an actor. Nothing else will do. You don't settle for less. The first test of whether you will be one is whether you have the strength to become one.'

For most actors, drama school or university are the first steps on what may be a very long ladder. There are some who feel that the slightly more academic route of the university drama course is for them. They may be persuaded by parents who are still clinging on to the hope that their child will choose a career that has job security, a defined path, and more important, is something with which they can identify. In the 1970s, taking a university drama course was seen as getting something to support you when the acting failed. Now, in the twenty-first century, we are all aware that a university degree is no guarantee of job security. In fact, the argument that acting is a precarious profession is not one that carries much weight when persuading people not to undertake it. In these times of economic uncertainty, many professions can be labelled precarious. At least as an actor, you know that tomorrow there's also a chance that the phone will ring; that the day might bring something new and amazing. If you're a plumber who has just been fired from a long, secure, in-house maintenance contract, the odds are much smaller that someone is going to ring you on the off-chance asking for a new ballcock.

For myself I always knew that the route was going to be drama school. My school were keen to push me to a university, not to read drama, but to do a subject that they felt was suitable for a Yorkshire red-brick grammar-school boy in the 1970s. I was Oxbridge material, so I was told, but what I was not told was that Oxford and Cambridge are as good a launching pad for a career in the theatre as a drama school. I was constantly told I should concentrate on having a viable career, and that plays and acting were for high days and holidays. These words were spoken to a seventeen-year-old who had just played the lead in the school's production of *Oh! What a Lovely War* and who had garnered praise from the *Rotherham Advertiser* and the *Sheffield Star* – words destined to fall on fallow ground. I managed to locate one dog-eared pamphlet in the school careers room entitled 'A Career in Drama'. Even this was focused on those who wanted to teach the subject, but it did mention where you could get information about drama schools.

I was offered a place at RADA eventually, but with this good news came the dawning realisation of just how wealthy my parents were not. Funding me through three years of a London drama school was quite simply not an option for them. In those days, if you wanted a grant from establishments such as RADA, Rotherham Borough Council set its own test. You auditioned for a matronly woman in a church hall on a Saturday afternoon who would assess your talent. It's a cause of immense irritation to me that I can no longer remember this woman's name, but I can remember her decision. I was not talented enough for a discretionary grant for a drama school. I applied for a scholarship from RADA. That was also not to be. However, I was not to be dashed upon the rocks. My passion still burned high enough. I discovered that with two A levels, and a place at Manchester Polytechnic School of Theatre, Rotherham Council were duty-bound to give me a grant. And that's exactly what happened.

If I had been trying to do the same thing in today's climate of student loans and a lack of grants, I am not sure I would have made it. These days, funding a training has to be even more imaginative for young people from low-income families. Scholarships do exist, but they are few and far between, and competition for them is stiff.

If you are a drama-school graduate, your struggle to get there was probably as hard or even more so than mine. To secure funding and a place to further your ambitions takes a great deal of hard work, even if there are family treasures that can be sold to pay for it. Though now there are more drama-school places open to aspiring actors than there has ever been, competition these days is increasingly fierce. You may have not been able to audition for all the drama schools of your choice. It can cost £1,000 or more to come to London and audition for five drama schools. The big six – RADA, Central, LAMDA, Guildhall, Bristol Old Vic and [insert your favourite sixth choice here] (Rose Bruford, Mountview, ArtsEd, East 15 and ALRA are all contenders) – will have most people auditioning for them. After that, you have to work your way through the rest of the list as appropriate. Drama schools have to operate as businesses. They have quotas to fill, and course fees to collect and, at £27,000-a-student for a three-year course, you're more than just a bundle of talent – you are a viable financial asset. Anyone who has sat through a drama-school final-year showcase knows that not everyone they see in it was chosen on grounds of talent alone. In some cases it's blindingly obvious that some of the people appearing were chosen for reasons other than their acting ability. Possibly the fact that they could bring £27,000 in student fees to the drama school.

Acting is not a quantifiable skill. There is no way to grade it. If there were, the whole process of casting would be made so much simpler. Casting agents would work their way through all the Grade Ones before moving down to the Grade Twos, or, in the case of many jobs, start by seeing something of the Grade Fours as they're probably the cheapest. Mercifully this is not the case. One man's Rylance is another man's Rylan – though I'm relishing the thought that by the time you read this the latter has fallen back into pre-*X Factor* obscurity. We are all allowed to pick our favourite. Which is what makes it difficult now that the drama schools are churning out so many people, year after year. Inevitably the number of actors who fall by the wayside in the first twelve to twenty-four months of their working lives has increased. It has become increasingly hard to cope with all the things you have to do to get work, over and above just being able to act.

British drama training is the best in the world. That's why we get so many foreign students wanting to come and train as actors here. Dreams that began in places as far apart as Alaska and Addis Ababa can both come to fruition within the hallowed halls of the British drama school. Drama-school training is constantly reinventing itself to fit the market. Yet even on a three-year full-time training course, time can be short. The days can be taken up with working on voice, movement, stage fighting, text work, characterisation and comedy, and suddenly there is no time to look at how you might sell yourself in the real world. Many of the more reputable drama schools include visits from professional casting directors and agents during the final year. They have talks from alumni who are making a career out of their training, but the very nature of the business means that you only really begin to learn what is needed once you have left drama school. Couple this with a little soupçon of inbuilt arrogance, which every actor needs to have, and it means that you think you are the person who is going to work. So you might suddenly be shocked when you confront what might be called 'the day the acting stops'.

And, of course, it's not only recent drama-school graduates that will have to confront this day. Actors confront it several times a year, when a job finishes. Even approaching the grand old age of sixty, if I finish a job and there's nothing else in the diary, I'm absolutely convinced that I will never work again. For a graduate, the day the acting stops is even more severe. For the past three years acting has been a vital ingredient of your day. Every morning you have woken up and gone to a building where acting has taken place. You've not had to question whether it will be part of your life. And yet, now, on this day, you're out in the wide world and the only way you'll ever act again is if you make it happen.

What you have to become is a 'Working Actor'. A person whose life is about being an actor. Because that is what everybody leaving college wants to do. They want to work, and for a very lucky small percentage that will indeed be the case. Sure enough, unemployment will figure in your life at some point, but just how do you minimise that?

This is absolutely the time to start planning. Business planning. Distinguishing between dreams and objectives. Looking at what is in your control, and what you can't change. If you were in any job, other than that of being a freelance actor, at the end of your first working year you would have an appraisal or assessment with your manager. They would examine just how successful you have been during that year, how you've improved, what objectives you have reached, and what you need to do to make the second year even more successful. As freelancers, you won't find such an appraisal or assessment in place. Yet how will you know whether you have been successful when that first year as an actor has gone by? When you are no longer the flavour of the month and next year's keen and eager graduates – blonder, younger, and possibly more talented than you – are flooding onto the market. How will you give yourself that edge when you are last year's model? It's this constant assessment of just how well you're doing, and what you've achieved, that can be the backbone of giving you both longevity and sustainability in your career. It can help give you the feeling of success that is so necessary to carrying on. It can, in extreme situations, also act as a pointer as to when it's probably wise to change paths. It will be very advantageous to take a look at creating one of these plans later in the book.

So how do you differentiate yourself as a young actor coming out of drama school? What are the things you can do to get attention? During the last couple of months of your course, your attention has all been on showcases, final productions, and probably the last thing you have thought about is getting a job. Indeed, during these final months it is easy to be much more focused on getting an agent than getting a job. It seems strange that you're suddenly prepared to put all your hopes and dreams into the hands of another person. The relationship with an agent, if you're lucky enough to get one, is key to getting work, but it's not the be all and end all of employment opportunities. Having struggled through a showcase and final-year shows, and having acquired an agent, you can't just turn off the search for work. You might have to turn it back on again some six or eight weeks later when you haven't had a single casting or meeting, but, of course, it's useful to be able to blame someone else – your agent!

Dealing with your agent, dealing with unemployment, dealing with feeling down, and dealing with the people you meet who might give you work are all key to your business.

But whether you're new to the world, having just left drama school or university, or whether you are several years into a career that has already had its highlights, and yet doesn't really seem to have settled down into anything regular, now is the time to start your Working Actor plan. Sometimes every new job can feel like a new start and achieving any sense of continuity in a career can be difficult. Let's begin that with the first of the work tasks below, and hopefully allow you to use the exercises, the ideas, the inspirations, the anecdotes, and at least some of the advice, contained in the following pages and turn yourself into a Working Actor.

Work Task

To record your progress, start a document on your computer, or a notebook, that is going to keep track of your work tasks.

Write down the five things that differentiate you from any other actor. Some of them may be things that work in tandem with each other. For example, I'm currently one of only two fifty-nine-year-old professional actors who were born in Rotherham. Now please don't tell anybody else that, but write down the differentiators for yourself.

What is it that *you* bring into the room that is hard to find from anyone else? Don't think of things like punctuality or discipline – these are expected of all actors.

What is your casting type? Age, social class, character qualities. The more defined this is, the easier it is to hit the right targets.

2. Spotting opportunities

Maximising the number of opportunities available to you is the principal way of improving the amount of work that you will get. Leaving drama school, where training is still primarily focused on the stage, means many people are focused on a theatre job as being 'proper work'. Increasingly, it is in television that young actors will get their first paid role. There are many areas, though, where your skills as an actor can be employed that you may not have thought of. So let's create a breakdown of potential employment areas, and then begin to talk through them.

Using young or recently graduated actors as a focus is one way of looking at what is out there. Drama UK recently commissioned an innovative piece of research on graduate destinations. The 2012 graduates from the three-year acting course at nineteen drama schools had their employment tracked. Ian Kellgren, Chief Executive of Drama UK, said:

'This detailed research is the start of a major project in establishing a keen understanding of the employment landscape for actors. This is very important in helping to protect our world-class industry by providing it with the skilled workforce it needs. It also gives an understanding of the range of opportunities for performers and the challenges in equipping and supporting them for these.'

I'm grateful to Ian and Jude Tisdall at Drama UK, and Jane Deitch who conducted the research on their behalf, for allowing me to draw on the findings of the survey to create a picture of the current employment landscape.

This survey broke down the employment destinations that actors could currently find themselves in into two categories:

- **Recorded media:** television, film, radio, internet, commercial and voice.

- **Live media:** theatre, entertainment, dance and music-based projects.

In each of those categories, there are, of course, many subdivisions. The figures that back up Jane Deitch's research are interesting. In the year 2012/13 (students graduating in the summer of 2012), a total of 474 graduates had their employment tracked. These graduates produced a total of 1,697 'jobs'. 365 of these graduates (77%) had representation from an agent, and 427 of them (90%) were in Spotlight, which is considered to be the main casting directory of the profession. What the research makes clear is that doesn't mean that each graduate had a total of 3.58 jobs! Some were much luckier than others. The research doesn't tell us the percentage of work for actors with agents, as opposed to those who were unrepresented, but in line with current perception, it is more than likely that most of the television work went to actors who have agents.

Recorded media

A total of 710 jobs, or 42% of the work that was under-taken by these graduates, took place in what has been identified as recorded media.

Television

The survey shows 195 television jobs for UK graduates in 2012–13. 93 commercials, 36 internet virals, 31 radio, 39 voice-over jobs and 38 jobs in categories covering music videos, video games and others. In this digital age, and with the proliferation of television channels, it might have been thought that the employment opportunities for actors would increase greatly. That has not necessarily been the case. The huge amount of material that does not require acting talent (reality television, foreign imports, game shows and fly-on-the-wall documentaries) has ensured that opportunities for actors in drama or comedy-based entertainment on television has remained remarkably level for many years.

Television can seem to be the hardest sector for an actor to break into unless they have an agent. Casting briefs for television are very rarely released to public-access sites where all actors can see them. Most drama for BBC and ITV is now produced by independent companies. Most of these companies will use freelance casting directors on a project-by-project basis, so it is managing your relationship with a particular casting director that may bring you an opportunity to be seen for a television role if you don't have an agent. Occasionally when casting something difficult and with very particular physical, ethnic, or skill-based needs, the casting director on a major drama may release this information to one of the casting services. We'll take a look at those later.

Soap operas are often the flagship programmes of the channels that have one, and they all have resident casting directors working on them. The casting directors stay in place for various lengths of time on each of the soaps, but they may have a longer relationship with the programme. While they too may make agents their first port of call when casting new roles, they are a much better target to write to for the unrepresented actor. It is possible to write to them and send details which may be kept on file, as their casting needs are ongoing and not just project-related. Resident casting directors may be more effective in terms of someone with whom one can build up a relationship. The role of the casting director is key, and it is a function that frustrates as many actors as it helps. We will look at their role later, and also talk to them to find out what they feel that actors can do to increase their chance of gaining a job. The difficulty for most actors here is that the casting directors will prefer to conduct the relationship through an agent whenever possible.

The main change in television in this century has been the involvement of the public and the creation of reality media. Whereas, once upon a time, the nightly story of eight people sharing a house would have been a drama cast with and peopled by actors, now it is a gladiatorial arena for members of the public to interact with each other and try to win our approval. Many hours of programming that were once drama-based are now reality-drama-based. Many of these projects do advertise on the casting services, as well as on the television channel's own websites. They are not really a route for an actor. They are supposedly a road to fame, possibly fleeting, and rarely talent-based. You as an actor are looking for work that exercises your skills, and focusing on this is your main concern.

Work Task

Look through the *Radio Times*, either in print or online, or other online listings, and make a list of all the production companies that produce the sort of drama you feel you could be cast in. Then visit the website of each of these companies where you should be able to find a full list of the work they make, and a list of key personnel. Which of these productions will be making another series? Who is directing? Who will be casting it? There's nothing wrong with a professional business email to the company asking those questions. Keep a record of whom you have written to, at which company, and the response.

Film

Of the graduates, 64 had jobs in the type of film that you're likely to see at your local cinema on a Saturday afternoon, a major studio production, which, once again, will have been cast by a casting director, and might seem beyond reach to actors without agents. Whether these were leading roles, or the one- or two-line 'cameo' (as the small part is affectionately known), we have no figures. Casting directors on movies tend to go out in search of actors they have already thought of, actors whose work they know, or actors whose agents they have an existing relationship with, rather than use unsolicited suggestions. Several of the casting services publish generic information regarding what films may or may not be coming up into production. How correct this information might be is something you have to judge for yourself. Most of the casting for large features is done between casting directors and agents, and if you are currently without an agent, your efforts may be better focused on getting one than trying to get into the film world. Mercifully there are a large number of British independent films being made, many under the auspices of the BBC and Channel 4. From time to time you hear about the resurgence of the British film industry and how well it's doing, and it may be frustrating that you can't seem to break into it. If you haven't worked in film before, then you're probably going to need something on a showreel for your agent to interest people with, and that means you're going to need to boost your showreel somehow. 208 of the listed jobs from the graduate survey were for appearances in films termed as 'shorts'. All of this would be classified as paid work, even if paid at the Equity minimum salary for film-school work, which is below agreed salaries for film and television. Take at look at Chapter Four for more information on short films and how to use them as a stepping stone.

Radio/Voice-over

The voice-over or radio section of the workload seems to be surprisingly small. Of the 474 graduates and a total of 1,697 jobs, only 31 radio jobs and 39 voice-over engagements don't seem to present a great opportunity on the work front. I think we're safe in assuming here that the radio jobs are probably radio drama, and therefore almost certainly at the BBC, whereas voice-over jobs can cover everything from commercials, documentary narration, internet viral and instructional CDs. For the actor sitting at home, perhaps unrepresented, it's an area that is easy to make steps to get into. Thoughts on what is needed on a good voice reel are shared later in the book.

Live media

A higher graduate target was 987 jobs (or 58%) in live media. A live-media classification in this survey covered everything from West End appearances, regional repertory jobs, small-scale touring, commercial tours, international work, fringe and Off-West End productions, festivals, corporate jobs, workshops and rehearsed readings, and entertainment. That last category may have included such anomalies as the end-of-the-pier show in Cromer. It's hard to tell.

What is interesting to note is that nearly half of the live-media jobs – 424 – were in fringe and Off-West End shows. These are areas that are not only well suited to actors of lesser experience, but also great for actors who leave drama school unrepresented and need a further showcase to attract an agent. Add to this a further 164 jobs in workshops and rehearsed readings, and it's easy to see where young actors in the first few years of their career are aiming themselves. In comparison, at the other end of the theatre scale, 10 new graduate jobs were provided by the RSC, 7 by the National Theatre, 8 by the Royal Court, 4 by Shakespeare's Globe, 2 by the Donmar Warehouse and 1 by the Almeida. Again, the research doesn't tell us how many of these jobs were leading roles, and how many were small parts, or spear carriers. The important thing for the actor is most probably that it was a job.

One of the great benefits of this extensive research is that it allows young actors to focus on the areas of work that are most likely to provide opportunities at a particular point in their career. There is work out there, and by correctly targeting the job opportunities that are most suitable for yourself, your chances increase a great deal.

Work Task

Make a list of the theatres where, in an ideal world, you would like to work. Make sure that you not only include major companies whose work interests you, but find five fringe venues whose work you also like. Are there any fringe venues near you geographically? How could you get to know them? What are the sorts of jobs where you can realistically approach the company or venues yourself?

Check out the forthcoming programmes for all the theatres you've listed and try to find out what the casting requirements are for each play. Some larger theatre companies list casting requirements on their website. The Royal Exchange Theatre in Manchester is an excellent example of a company that does this. If you can't find that information on the website, then think about noting down the titles of the plays and spending an afternoon browsing in a bookshop or local library. I have spent many an hour in the excellent Samuel French's theatre bookshop in Fitzroy Street, London W1. They are quite used to actors coming in and sitting down and reading most of the plays, and many of their staff are exceptionally knowledgeable about the stock. The National Theatre has a fabulous bookshop by the banks of the Thames where it's possible to do the same thing. Check out your local theatre and see if it has a bookshop, or some of the larger libraries, who will also have excellent online catalogues and may order books in for you.

Now add the roles that you think you might be suitable for to the list of plays, and then find out the casting deadlines for those particular productions. Most plays at major theatres rehearse for at least four weeks, and tend to be cast around three to four weeks before rehearsals begin, so with the opening-date information that you gain from the website you should be able to get an idea when the casting process will take place.

Keep revising your list on a weekly or fortnightly basis. In terms of theatre, if you do find a role you feel is suitable that is coming up at a particular venue, don't be afraid of checking with your agent to see if you have been suggested.

3. Finding work

In order to get in the room for the interview, you need to be in the know – to be aware of what is casting and who is casting it. To do this, you need information. So just how do you get yourself in the know and get that vital info? You may feel that with your agent beavering away on your behalf, you are in the know. But is that really the case? Should you not also be keeping an eye on what is going on and working with your agent to increase the number of possible opportunities?

If you don't have an agent, then you need to get as much knowledge as possible about what is going on in terms of work. That information can come from a variety of sources. When I started out as a young actor in the 1970s, there were several ways of getting information. The main one was the profession's newspaper, *The Stage*. Following the principle taught to me by one of my tutors at drama school – 'Do one thing each day that might lead to work, and then get on with living your life' – my one thing on Thursday was to buy *The Stage*, or on the weeks when I couldn't afford it, to stand in WHSmith and scour the job pages. If I thought there was a job suitable for me to apply for, then I would hand over the necessary 40p (or some such ridiculously small amount), and take it home to write the letter.

There was also a subscription service known as Professional Casting Report, or PCR, which you could have sent to your home address once a week. This was a circular that came on red paper and purported to have up-to-the-minute and confidential cast information listed on it. Sometimes a group of us would subscribe together, and pass the red sheets round on Monday morning in a coffee bar to chase up the leads. Many of the leads came to nothing, and some of the information it contained was of dubious provenance, but for me as an out-of-work actor with no agent, any straw was to be clutched at.

For the actor without an agent who is looking for work, or for the actor with an agent who wants to keep busy and maximise their opportunities, the ways of getting information have remained essentially the same. What you will find is that there are more suppliers claiming to have information, or providing channels for you to contact potential employers. A quick check online will throw up many of them, and the problem you might have now is how to decide which of them is the best investment.

Several of the casting information services are essentially free if you are a member of another organisation. Equity has a job information service on its website, and Spotlight has a casting information service which circulates to its members. *The Stage* now has a casting information service as well as its job adverts, but it does require a separate subscription.

You will also find casting information services that will provide you with everything from a website to a means of directly suggesting yourself for jobs. Websites like CastNet, Casting Call Pro, StarNow and Mandy.com all aim to increase the number of opportunities you will have for gaining work. I took the opportunity to talk to several of the casting services to find out what they feel they can do for you, how they do it, and what casting professionals feel about them.

There are now so many casting services that it would be impossible to keep track of all of them. You would need to be earning a good salary in order to pay for subscriptions to them all, so just how do you choose between them, and indeed what, if anything, can they do for you?

Equity job information service

The best thing about the Equity job information service is, of course, that it's free if you are an Equity member. Unsurprisingly it's the page that gets the most hits on the Equity website. Equity has a strict policy that only paid work is advertised. You can log into the job information service on the Equity website using your membership number, and available jobs can be selected by keywords, by gender, from one of the following sectors – Acting, Dance, Non-performing, Singing, Variety/ Circus/Light Entertainment.

After selecting a sector, you will see the list of available jobs according to your criteria. A single line or two describes a job and there is a link for you to click on to read more about what is required. On the next page is a more comprehensive description of requirements, and pay and terms are clearly listed. Usually there will be an email address that you can apply to, and some guiding criteria that you should use for your application. Equity ask you to follow this, and the fact that most people do means that people still submit jobs to the website. Equity relies on its members to use common sense, a rare demand made on actors, and apply for things that they are suitable for, rather than imposing any electronic filters. The decision is in your hands.

On the day that I clicked on the job service to investigate what was available, and wanting to push the envelope a little bit, I selected male and actor. I found the work available was a schools tour, a children's party presenter, voice tutors for work in drama schools and in Saturday stage schools, a mid-scale tour of *The Princess and the Pea*, a workshop and Christmas production of *The BFG* being put together by Birmingham Rep, and a very small-scale tour of an Ibsen play paying £350 a week, lodging and breakfast, but no subsistence.

It was an eclectic mix, and certainly one that you would have to sift through. Being realistic, you're not going to find television or film work on this site, unless it's a good student film (and these can be exceptionally useful), or a television casting brief which is proving difficult to cast due to its specificity, i.e. the casting director is looking for a particular disability, or minority group.

You won't find underpaid fringe opportunities on this site due to Equity's policies, but it's certainly worth checking out as it could throw up opportunities you haven't yet thought of.

All in all, the job service is a useful point of contact with information and job requirements that you might not otherwise find. It's free as an Equity member and it's updated daily and backed by the union. It's also great for sources of information about non-performing jobs for getting through the down times. It's highly unlikely that you'll find any top television castings on here, or on any open-information source, as casting directors don't want to be flooded by unsuitable applications.

Work Task

The Equity job service updates daily and, as with all leads, getting an early application in never harms your chances. Why not put a time of day into your diary to check the job information service. Other casting services may send alerts when suitable work comes in, but with the Equity job service, the onus is on you to check it. Bookmark the page on your phone, or on your iPad or computer.

Spotlight

Spotlight is 'the home of casting' – that's one of its slogans. 'Professional acting jobs and auditions since 1927' is proudly displayed on its website. As an actor, you need Spotlight. I would suggest that there is absolutely no argument as to that. Spotlight's remit, as I was told by Pippa Harrison, head of client relations, is to get its members as many quality casting opportunities as possible. Spotlight is the way that you market yourself as an actor. If you were a plumber, you would be in *Plumber's World* or *Yellow Pages*. If you're an actor, you're in Spotlight. It's part of being an actor. As a small business, which is, of course, what you are, your marketing budget should certainly include your Spotlight subscription, because that is how you make sure that you are on the desk of every casting director who is looking for professional actors. You are now part of the vast database that is Spotlight, and casting directors doing specific searches can find you.

Historically, Spotlight was a collection of weighty tomes that graced the shelves of any casting director's office. Several alphabetically compiled books for male actors, and a similar set for actresses, as they were called then. You had an ad in the books and it was all about being found. More recently, Spotlight has been at the forefront of the digital casting service with the Spotlight Link, where casting directors can search for actors and send information to their agents and to Spotlight members on specific jobs. 90% of the work cast in the UK goes out on the Spotlight Link. Hardly surprising, then, that the directory has over 60,000 members.

If you went to an accredited drama school, you were probably introduced to the service through the student Spotlight, and then became a member of the big directory without actually thinking what Spotlight could do for you. 1,200 graduates from approximately twenty-one schools join the student Spotlight every year. If you didn't attend a course at an accredited drama school, or came through the university route, then Spotlight would want to see four verifiable professional credits before allowing you to become a member. The Spotlight vetting process is one of the strictest of any of the casting services, but that is because it wants casting directors to know it is the place to find professional actors. Trained professional actors. There are many who regard having a Spotlight page as your professional badge. Dames Judi Dench and Helen Mirren, Sir Anthony Hopkins – none of them need a Spotlight page in order to get work, and yet they all have them. It's a Kitemark of your existence and credibility as a Working Actor.

As an actor with representation, any suitable casting briefs from Spotlight will be sent directly to your agent. Casting directors submitting work on the service can choose to whom they distribute the information. They can select to send a brief to all agents, or they can select to send to specific agents, or they can just select to send the information to one agent. They can also choose to release the information to actors who don't have agents, who are often listed 'c/o The Spotlight'. What this means in real terms is that Spotlight will manage any enquiries on your behalf and forward them to you by phone, email, or SMS.

Actors who don't have agents can also take advantage of the Spotlight casting information service. All job briefs that have not been limited by the casting director to specific agents are published by the service and, depending on the filters that you have put in place – age, accent, height, nationality, etc. – relevant briefs will be forwarded to you. You can still see these briefs if you are registered with Spotlight with an agent, but you won't actually be able to submit yourself in order to prevent the casting director from receieving the same submission from both you and your agent. You can either contact your agent and ask whether you have been submitted for a particular job, or you can rely on their judgement as to whether they have suggested you for it. As actors, we aren't always the best judges of what we should be suggested for.

The most impressive thing about the Spotlight casting information service is the sheer wealth of castings that it lists. When I looked at the site, on a random hot afternoon in July, people were looking for a dad for an Argos commercial, a keep-fit man for a Channel 4 short, a French-accented man for a corporate video, and actor-dancers for a UK tour of Barry Manilow's *Copacabana*.

On the link board of the Spotlight casting service you can click on all casting briefs that match your filters, all paid jobs, or you can click on something labelled as 'all opportunities'. Spotlight classes many low-paid jobs – i.e. jobs that are being paid at a rate below the Equity minimum, or profit-share or unpaid jobs – as 'opportunities'. It fully supports the Equity guidelines on low-paid and no-paid work, but thinks that its members should be allowed the chance to make up their own minds if they want to invest their time in an opportunity that's on offer that may bring them further work. To ensure that members are not being exploited, at the bottom of each casting brief you will now find a button labelled 'Report concern'. This allows members to report back to Spotlight any concerns they have once they have followed up the casting brief that has been published. It means that Spotlight can withdraw the listing in an instant should it be necessary.

One major criticism of the system for actors without agents is that the information you receive for your subscription will be more limited than that which is sent out to agents. This is the choice of the casting directors, although Pippa Harrison at Spotlight did tell me that the service does encourage casting directors to circulate the information as widely as possible on as many occasions as they can. Given that Spotlight vets all its members to such a high degree, casting directors can be sure that, even if they send out information to actors without agents, they are sending it out to actors who have been trained or have professional credits. This is where Spotlight, the brand, really begins to deliver for you. Unless they definitely want to find themselves dealing with members of the public, casting directors tend to use Spotlight as the first port of call for casting their net as wide as possible. If they are looking for unrepresented actors to fit a specific brief (height, build, ethnicity), and that can quite often be the reason that they are not dealing with agents, then they still want to make sure that they are getting trained, professional actors.

It's very easy to think that having paid your subscription and submitted your CV and photograph, that's the end of it – and you can just sit back and wait for the auditions to roll in. If that is all you do, then you're not taking advantage of an enormous number of resources that you have paid for by taking out a Spotlight membership.

You can call into the Spotlight office for careers advice and a chat. Career Mondays are a service that Spotlight offers where members can make an appointment to chat with their career adviser for a twenty-minute slot. You know that being an actor can be a very lonely profession. More often than not, you don't have any co-workers. You don't have anyone you share your office with. You're isolated a lot of the time. You can go and work with a group of people for six or eight weeks, and then never see them again. You need to have a very strong ego to withstand that, and this is where the support side of Spotlight comes into play. The team at Spotlight know the industry very well. Spotlight is not an agent. It is not a casting director. It has no set agenda. Often actors just need somebody to unload to, someone who will tell you that you're doing the right things, and that you are following the right path. Someone to check that you're match fit and you're networking, and you're going to the theatre. The people at Spotlight can't wave a magic wand, but they can and will give you time.

Spotlight has stayed well ahead in terms of digital development, with a huge investment in programming technology to enable its services to be truly state-of-the-art. In its turn this has produced a lot of online resources which you, the member, are able to use.

You should check the Spotlight website closely. You can find discounts on a huge variety of services and goods all related to being a performer, such as subscriptions to *The Stage*, headshots, gym membership, even teeth whitening. Clever use of these discounts can actually make your Spotlight subscription pay for itself. The website contains a huge amount of career advice in the form of podcasts and articles available for members to listen to and download, with a huge range of advice from casting directors and industry professionals.

July 2014 saw the launch of Spotlight's upload service, which will surely play a great part in the widespread use of self-taping for first rounds of interviews. At first-round interviews now, it is almost assured that you won't meet the director, and increasingly likely that you won't meet the casting director either. The interview will be placed on tape by an assistant. Given the increase in readily available technology, such as the iPhone, it now becomes a real possibility that actors could self-tape their first-round audition and submit it. We'll look at more about how you can do this well and make it work for you later in this book.

The image that many people have of Spotlight is a set of huge volumes languishing on a bookshelf, and indeed Spotlight do still produce a printed edition of the directory. Evidently a lot of casting directors quite like having the books, but the book is only printed on demand. These days it is the online services that Spotlight has invested in so heavily that give it the edge, and make it a must-have marketing tool for any actor who is taking work seriously.

Once you begin to look at the huge wealth of services that Spotlight offers, other than just holding your picture on its casting directory, the value-for-money of that subscription becomes increasingly apparent. After an afternoon spent investigating the website to look at all these other services, I began to wonder how you can exist as an actor with any level of credibility unless you feature in Spotlight. Leaving the office in Leicester Place I noticed the following quote on the wall.

'Spotlight must be considered by all in the profession as an invaluable asset. I am no different from anyone else; I use it all the time.'

Sir Laurence Olivier

I have a picture in my head of Sir Laurence's page in Spotlight. Just a photo and his name. No credits, just that imposing godlike image making him available for employment to the world... Perhaps that's how he ended up in the 1980s version of *Clash of the Titans*. There can't be any other explanation. What he says, however, still stays true today. Spotlight is a resource that no working actor can do without, but you may just want to check that you're getting the maximum benefit out of your subscription. It's not cheap, but it's certainly worthwhile, with lots of hidden perks and features that might not be apparent at first glance. Take time to have a look and make the most of your subscription.

Work Task

Set aside an hour and log into Spotlight. You can have a good look round if you are not a member and see what is on offer. If you already have a subscription, then using your pin code, log into the casting service and make sure that the filters that define the roles which are sent to you are correct. Check the age, height, and type of role. Update your CV, and check that your photographs are up to date, and your showreel is also uploaded. Spotlight is a great place to have a couple of different photographs – the main one displayed will be, by default, the one that is printed in the Spotlight directory.

Look through all the podcasts and articles that are available to you as a Spotlight member. You will find several of an exceptionally practical nature. Download a podcast to listen to on your journey to whatever you're doing the following day.

Take a good look at the discounts and offers available to you on the website, such as insurance, or gym membership, and try to take advantage of these money-saving perks of membership. If necessary, save the page as a PDF and store it on your computer, or print it out for your noticeboard so that you can have easy reference to it, or write down the date for any relevant offers.

If you're thinking of having new photographs for the next edition, note down the day for your Spotlight renewal and put a reminder in your diary six weeks before. By doing this, you can prepare, both financially and administratively, so that taking advantage of this first-class casting and marketing tool does not take you by surprise.

CastNet

I spoke to Will Wollen, who is a consultant for CastNet. The main thing that struck me was his passion about what he is doing and how CastNet works. In my view, that's always a good starting point. CastNet first started its online submission service in 1998 and was the first service to get off the ground on the internet. It started as a reaction to the way that actors without agents were being, as Will put it, 'kept from work'. CastNet used to use postal services, and also used to do the letters and submissions on behalf of actors, so it has a good understanding of the business. As I believe all casting services should, CastNet has criteria for membership for people wishing to use the service. You need to have completed a course at an accredited training establishment, or you need significant professional experience (meaning at least three professional paid jobs). Should you meet the criteria, and they do check, then at the time of writing, fees for CastNet vary between £3.95 a week for the standard service and up to £6.50 a week for the premium service. There is a free service, and this is open to non-professionals, but it gives no information on paid work. You can take a break from the service when in work, and take payment holidays when you need to.

The premium service allows you to customise your CV for different applications. I think that's absolutely crucial in focusing your CV and leading with appropriate credits for the job you are applying for. People receiving television submissions rarely want to wade through a long list of theatre credits first, and vice versa. The premium service also gives you the chance to upload unlimited media and headshots to your CastNet page. As a premium member you also get the chance to create your own personal website. Log in and you can combine lots of the templates to give you customisation options. As part of my research, Will set up a trial membership for me, and I found the creation of my CastNet website to be remarkably simple and effective. You could also buy a domain name for yourself from a web company and then have this link through to your CastNet website and page. Your premium CastNet page also gives you document storage, which is exceptionally useful for storing CVs and biographies for different jobs.

Someone searching for you as an actor online will come across your CastNet page, and the service is free to casting directors logging in. As the casting professional logs in, they will see the 'Meet an Actor' feature that introduces them to new members of CastNet. 92% of actors on CastNet have agents, but these actors see the value in chasing the work themselves. The casting breakdowns and suggestions you will get from CastNet are tailored to you. This is dependent on the information that you have entered into your profile, but the more specific you make your profile, the better the casting information that arrives in your inbox.

CastNet is definitely for actors as opposed to some of the other services which do seem to be tailored for the 30,000 teenagers who have just watched *The Voice*. Will says that the service has definitely got him work. 'Nice bits of telly. It's got me work directly. It's got me work indirectly, giving me information that I wouldn't otherwise have had.'

Will was a great proponent for the services of CastNet, but does it actually work in reality? I tried it both as a casting director, and as an actor. I put out a casting brief for a small corporate video that I was casting. The suggestions I got back were good, clear, and appropriate. The covering email message sent with the submissions from the actors was in some cases a little unspecific, but this was more down to the failing of the actor to express themselves and their suitability correctly, rather than with any mismatch on the CastNet system. The corporate casting brief that I put out had a very tight timeline as I needed suggestions within a couple of hours. I was very impressed that, within half an hour of putting the submission onto CastNet, someone from the site had contacted me to check the details and make sure that everything went out as I wanted it to.

The main reason why casting directors prefer to contact agents, rather than use a casting service and contact actors, is that they can find themselves at the mercy of when the actors themselves decide to check their information or their email. An agent's office is constantly manned and can provide a response reasonably quickly, particularly if the words 'availability check' or 'work' are in the email subject box. Even with this brief – a corporate one, the type of job about which agents used to be remarkably snooty – the first suggestion I had back on my desk was from an agent, rather than from a casting service. So if you are going to make CastNet work for you, then you do have to make sure that you are checking your emails on a regular basis. And by regularly, I mean at least hourly.

The quality of the brief that you are sent very much depends on the amount of detail and the precision of information you enter into your profile. I'm not sure my trial profile was as comprehensive as it needed to be for CastNet to work as effectively as it should. If I were asked to describe my own casting type, I think I would say late fifties, tall, authoritative, grumpy and native Yorkshire. (I should just point out here that grumpy doesn't always go with native Yorkshire but I have found it to be an effective combination.) One of the casting briefs I was sent asked for 'a fragile and a nerdish type who essentially projects fear in his eyes'. It went on to say more about 'this former priest, working for a small division of the CIA concerning the paranormal abroad. Although a man of science, he was evidently still a believer, since six years ago, he had been following a trail of infanticides that leave behind dim handprints of an ancient demon.'

It all sounded like what I do every day! I'd like to think that I could push the envelope and get near to 'fragile and nerdish', but I'm a realist. I'm from Rotherham. I'm not even sure I can spell the words, let alone portray them. I know there are hundreds of actors who would answer that description much better than me, and I have to say I was surprised to find that sort of role in my inbox. It may well have been the fault of the information I provided, or it may well have been as a result of a lack of specific targeting on the part of the people who submitted it. It may also have been as part of a desire to get as much information in front of as many actors as possible, it's hard to say. The notifications of castings have been reasonably regular, and regular information coming into your inbox does make you feel in the swing of things. Casting directors I spoke to said that they do use CastNet, but mainly when they have exhausted all other avenues.

There was one aspect of CastNet which did worry me slightly. Every ten days or so I received something called 'Production Notices'. This was a sheet of information about up-and-coming projects. Many of the projects only had a title and the production company attached, and were in the very early stages of pre-production, which is in the stages before they needed actor involvement. Certainly they were in the pre-casting stages, and on many of them a casting director had yet to be assigned. It is possible to look at this information as keeping CastNet members in the picture as to what is going on, but when you're out of work it can be difficult to resist the temptation to drop someone a letter which, unbeknownst to you, might not be well received.

CastNet seems to acknowledge this as their production notices do have a rider attached to them declaring that all the projects are in an early stage of development and that casting needs have not yet been identified. It points out clearly that the production company has not invited submissions and advises actors not to send CV and photograph at this stage. They ask that, if you do write to the company, you do not mention CastNet as the source of your information.

That's all pretty fair and yet I wondered how many people ignore that, and think that they are stealing an early march on the competition by getting their details in or expressing an interest in the project as a result of this. I personally would prefer it if the information was restricted to ongoing casting requirements rather than future possibilites. Just a personal opinion, but it may stop you writing an unsolicited letter and irritating a busy casting director or producer.

I would have to say that, on the whole, I was rather impressed by CastNet, and its ability to understand what actors want in a casting service. In addition to the fact that the lowest level of paid membership gets you what, in effect, is a rather classy website, the ease-of-use of the service, and the quality of the support, would seem to be worth the investment – lots of bells and whistles. It is a significant investment; even the standard level of membership works out more expensive than Spotlight, although it should be remembered that with both a standard membership and the premium membership, you are effectively getting your own personal website and other facilities too.

Work Task

Try out a basic free profile on CastNet and see what it looks like. Would this be of use to you? If you don't have a website, this is certainly an option worth considering.

The Stage

The Stage has come late to the arena of online casting information. It would seem that the digital world was not on the radar for *The Stage* until around 2009. Traditionally the back pages of *The Stage* were the place where actors would look for jobs. *The Stage* was the only medium that held job adverts for actors. Now, of course, the world has changed. Information is quickly and freely disseminated and no one is prepared to wait for one publication to appear on a Thursday.

So where is *The Stage* in the casting services market? I spoke to Grant Attwell, who is head of marketing at the newspaper. Grant acknowledges that *The Stage* is not trying to be a new Spotlight as far as casting information goes. Readership surveys through the newspaper found that their readership was the aspirational actor. In its casting service, therefore, *The Stage* offers more open-access jobs – jobs that are open to anyone. The newspaper itself has been a great advocate in the fight against no-pay and low-paid jobs, but acknowledges the fact that many young actors see this work as an opportunity. You can sign up to *The Stage*'s casting service for general alerts for free, which will give you information on profit-share and low-paid jobs, but if you want to get all the information that the service carries you need to become a subscriber. That doesn't mean a subscriber to the newspaper – whereas, with Spotlight, if you are a subscriber to the book you also can take advantage of the casting service, as a subscriber to *The Stage* newspaper, you don't get the added advantage of its casting service as well. They are separate entities. At the time of writing the subscription costs £10 a month or £100 a year. This allows you to apply for paid work advertised on the service. The subscription is flexible so that you can drop out when you are in work.

Spotlight is the home for trained actors. *The Stage* is as easily recognised and as strong a brand as Spotlight within the profession, and yet on its casting service it has no vetting process for people who wish to apply, so if you are a casting director looking for a trained actor, *The Stage* casting service might not be your first port of call. You won't find premium television castings listed here, or probably even repertory-theatre castings. You will find low-budget jobs, and jobs where the rates of pay are low, so many Equity members would not take them.

The Stage is read as avidly by amateurs throughout the United Kingdom as it is by professionals, and in these days of the *Britain's Got Talent* culture, with more people aspiring to make the crossover from amateur to professional without undergoing the training process, *The Stage*, and now its casting service, might be the first place they look.

Casting directors using the service obviously know that the roles they are advertising may well be sent out to untrained actors, but for them this is a good way to access that part of the market. They know that in the age of reality television, producers and directors are increasingly aware of other sources of potential cast members for their programmes. 12,000 people have signed up to the service very quickly, and it should get stronger. I looked at an advertisement in an online edition of the newspaper for the casting service. 7 jobs were paid jobs, 6 jobs were profit-share, and 3 jobs were unpaid or voluntary. That might be how *The Stage* sees the service, but, looking back over fourteen days during one month, 8 jobs listed were profit-share, 12 jobs listed were voluntary, 1 job was listed as expenses only and there were only 5 paid jobs listed.

The Stage casting service has a lot to do. Grant told me that it was listing between 25 and 50 jobs a week, but that is quite a low figure in comparison to the other services. The ability to take in online auditions will keep the service apace with Spotlight, and help actors with the growing trend of self-taping. Something slightly less exciting is the fact that it will provide a whole range of licensed backing tracks for audition videos. It all sounded a bit like online karaoke to me, but given that the service's biggest listing period is when pantomimes are being cast in July and August, it will certainly prove a useful service for anyone looking to get work in this area. Again, it could eliminate expensive and pointless first-round auditions if used properly.

Any casting service is only as good as the information it gets, and it seems that in this area *The Stage* is lacking. Why would a casting director use this service to look for trained actors when they have Spotlight at their fingertips? They may well use it if they're looking to extend the range of their casting outside people who call themselves actors for a living. That is of no real use to you, a trained actor looking to put your training into practice.

The Stage is the trade journal of the acting profession. It's absolutely first class for news and it is the industry bible. It gives you an understanding of the profession. The newspaper used to be called *The Stage and Television Today*. These days it is proud to be called *The Stage*, and as a result is much more theatre-focused and has become the mouthpiece of the theatre profession. Whereas websites such as WhatsOnStage.com carry news about what is going on in the theatre world, they do focus it rather more on the audience's perspective. *The Stage* still sees itself as an industry newspaper and it is a brand that people trust, certainly for its information. *The Stage* reviews used to be thought of as being there purely for information only, i.e. who is in the play, who's directed it, and where is it on. Popular parlance among actors used to acknowledge that the three most useless things in the world were 'the Pope's balls and a good notice in *The Stage*'. The newspaper is dealing with this. It now has two permanent critics, Mark Shenton and Natasha Tripney, and it's introduced a series of ratings on its reviews. These days, we are all very keen to merit a mention in *The Stage*.

So while the casting service may not yet deserve four stars, the newspaper certainly does. You can get a digital edition downloaded to your iPad on Thursday mornings with video content, click-through advertising and a whole host of informative and engaging features. If theatre is your world, then whether you get it online, or prefer that walk down to the newsagent as part of your routine, *The Stage* is like a trusted old friend who knows what's going on. And you can still stand in WHSmith and have a quick glance through for nothing.

Casting Call Pro

The next major casting service I looked at was Casting Call Pro. I spoke to Abigail Longstaffe, who is their industry liaison manager. Her job is to go out and build Casting Call Pro's connections with casting directors and encourage more agencies to start using the site and submitting actors through it.

Casting Call Pro is just one of a huge number of affiliated sites run by a company called Blue Compass. Dancers Pro, Singers Pro, Stage Jobs Pro, Entertainers Pro, Voices Pro, Promo Jobs Pro and the possibly misnamed Total Talent are all companies under the umbrella of Blue Compass. I have to say that by the time I got to the end of the list of these companies I was half expecting to see Talented Gerbils Pro, but evidently that's a market they've not yet tapped into.

Casting Call Pro was set up in 2004 and is the biggest of all the sites. Blue Compass Ltd, the parent company, are not such a recognised brand in the entertainment casting industry as Spotlight and *The Stage*, and are possibly an example of a technology company who came into the market due to the digital revolution and the way casting information is now disseminated. The sites are obviously a success as Abigail tells me they currently have 60,000 members. Drama students graduating from an accredited drama school get three months' free membership so they can try out the site and see how it works for them. Once the three months are finished then it's £20 a month or £156 a year, slightly more costly than Spotlight. Like several of the other sites, you can pay for a few months, stop your membership while you're away working, and then resume on your return.

Everyone gets a month's free trial, then as a standard member (that means somebody who has signed on for free), you can apply for everything classed on the site as 'opportunities', which is basically anything that is fringe work, profit-share, student films or underpaid, i.e. all work displayed is at less than the national minimum wage. As a premium member (someone who is paying), you can add multiple photographs and you can upload showreels and attachments as often as you like. You will receive all suitable opportunities that casting directors have submitted that match your filter, and, as a premium member, this will include paid work.

Casting Call Pro also organises surgeries for members with established professionals. You can book a fifteen-minute slot with someone to get one-to-one advice on headshots, CVs, and your career. Very valuable.

Casting Call Pro don't monitor actors' submissions, and they just ask that people think about what they are submitting themselves for. Casting directors getting lots of unsuitable submissions tend not to be pleased with the source. CCP did used to monitor suggestions where casting director requirements were very specific, but they no longer do this.

Casting directors will only continue to circulate information to casting sites when they feel the service is giving them relevant suggestions. Actors are not always the best people to decide what they should be cast as. In days of yore when casting submissions were sent in a manila 10'x8" envelope to the director's address, I have had submissions where, having asked for 'a 6'2" blond man, physically able to lift people, with a good sense of comedy,' I have heard from lots of 5'6" brunette guys saying: 'I'm not sure about the lifting, but I know I can play the part.' Hope is a great part of every actor's life, but knowing your suitability is another.

Casting Call Pro does seem to be the giant of the new casting services. Statistics provided from their own survey say that CCP provided five paid auditions per actor during 2013. Nearly half of their members have been contacted directly by an employer for work and 50% of those contacts had led to work. Out of 45,000 members, 1,790 responded to the Casting Call Pro survey. 50% of that number, i.e. 2% of all subscribers, were the people who said that those contacted led to work – just to show that you have to be beware of statistics posted on a company's own site.

Given that CCP is one of a huge network of sites under the same umbrella, what worries me is that they are more concerned with getting subscriptions than they are with actually getting work for actors. Most of the casting directors I spoke to said they would only use Casting Call Pro if they were looking to extend the range of their search outside what they would class as formally trained actors, so as an actor, a trained actor, you have to evaluate just how good a source of information it will be. Given that there are many free sources of information available, and that Casting Call Pro is probably one of the more expensive sites, it's a decision that should take some thought.

StarNow

I had heard of StarNow before I started doing this research, and I have to say the name put me off. It sounds like a Saturday-night television programme. Actually, it's probably the largest of the casting services that we've looked at yet, with three million members. It is a worldwide service based in New Zealand. Perhaps my initial reaction is that, even in the virtual world, how effective is that for getting a job in Manchester? In the UK alone StarNow has nearly 128,000 active members. But there is no application criteria for listing on the site. You must be over eighteen years to create your own profile, but applications may be submitted on behalf of minors by their parent or guardian. This is the go-to-for-everything casting superstore. Reality television, quiz-show contestants, short films, unpaid opportunities... so I doubt that it is the first port of call for casting professionals seeking trained actors. Its database is enormous and StarNow's stated vision is to be 'the biggest talent community on earth' and to 'simply provide quality casting choices that gets our talent discovered'. I was also told that StarNow has a set of company values and every employee aims to live these every day. I'm not sure what that says about the effectiveness of its role in the casting process, but it told me that this is an organisation with a large corporate mentality. It's not an organisation that came out of an existing casting brand. In fact, its origins lie in a very popular website known as Trade Me, which is New Zealand's equivalent of eBay.

StarNow has over 2,000 casting calls on its website every week, but you need to look at how many of these calls are actually of value to people based here in the UK in order to get an idea of its true worth. Membership costs around £60 a year (at the time of writing – I think you even have to sign up just to find out how much it costs), but there's no way to put this membership on pause while you're working. It's a little over a pound a week, which makes it much cheaper than many of the other UK-based services. It is also free to create a basic membership with StarNow and this will allow you to see every opportunity on site. They also email free members to let them know about new opportunities being listed that match their experience. StarNow feel that it is very much up to them to prove to their members, or 'the talent', as they call them, that they have great opportunities before customers subscribe. As with some of the other services, they have a blog, an extensive help section, and a video education section called 'The Edge', which is free and accessible for non-members. A lot of the information on here is from international sources and so not particularly relevant to you as a British actor, but the good thing is that you can access these vlogs without having to be a member of the site.

StarNow work closely with Surviving Actors in the UK and have a stand at each major event that Surviving

Actors run, in order to allow StarNow members to meet staff in person and ask them questions about how they work. Recently at a Surviving Actors event in Manchester, StarNow worked with the producers of a feature film entitled *Shooting Clerks* and held an open audition. Actors were seen on a first-come first-served basis (never something that I believe is a guarantee of quality), and the aim was to cast as many roles as possible from this open call. It's hard to find out if that happened, but I suspect that is unlikely. They may have cast many of the smaller supporting roles on their Manchester visit.

Though I was put off initially by the name, and interestingly enough I was told by one of the marketing directors that if they were launching now they probably wouldn't have used it, there is no doubt that StarNow is a hugely professional and international organisation. The resources on the website are a little diluted by the fact that the advice in this area is reasonably country-specific. The way that people approach agents in America probably wouldn't go down very well over here in the UK. The site is well priced, given the enormous number of members, but are you going to get lost on such a database? It's hard enough for most UK actors competing on their own shores, without spending money to compete with actors throughout the whole world.

Casting Networks

Casting Networks has been operating in the UK for just over three years, but it's no newcomer in the market. In the US it's been online for eleven years and is one of the most popular and well-used systems. It's backed by an incredible software programme that allows casting directors to select actors, create schedules, run auditions, transfer their material to the director, all within the Casting Networks interface. So if you, as an actor, have a profile on Casting Networks, then they can get your information directly from it. If you don't, then the casting director may still use the programme, but may put in an empty space for actors who don't have profiles on that system. This means that, at the end of the process, if the director is viewing the audition tapes through the Casting Networks system, and is sufficiently interested in an actor to see extra material, with a subscriber to Casting Networks all they would have to do is click on their profile and any extra material, such as a short showreel or photographs, they have uploaded would be instantly available. If the actor doesn't have a profile on the system, then the director has to get in touch with the casting director who has to get in touch with the agent to get the extra material sent over. They may do this, but in situations such as commercial castings where things are left to the last minute, it may be the difference between choosing one actor and the other.

Casting Networks is free for casting directors, and the system accredits casting directors before they are allowed access to it. Casting directors submit briefs primarily to agents, but they are being encouraged to use the casting billboard – the open-access part of the system. If you're an actor with representation then a basic profile is free on Casting Networks. Unrepresented actors pay a registration fee which is to ensure that they keep their profile active. You can buy add-ons: unlimited media hosting allows you to attach not only showreels, but individual clips from filmed appearances which can be attached to particular credits on the system. The language and action clips can be attached to your CV.

Casting Networks is pushing what's possible in the market. When they arrived and set up here, preceded by their reputation from America, they were probably the one company that Spotlight were worried about. It's only in the UK market that one casting service, Spotlight, has such a dominance. In the US, Casting Networks is just one of many services that are used and to which actors subscribe. The advantage of Casting Networks being a global company is that they make their money worldwide. They don't have to turn a profit in every market all the time, so they can invest in order to increase their presence, and this is certainly what they are intending to do. Casting Networks have a very competitive pricing strategy and you pay for the extra services that you need, such as radio and media upload. It is possible to have a good profile with photographs and media on this service for around £50, and that could make it a game-changer. Spotlight fees have not come down at all, even though they now only produce the printed books on demand.

The main downside to me of Casting Networks is that it has no entry criteria for people who register. A supermarket worker could register as an actor just as easily as someone who has graduated from LAMDA. (Not that I have anything against supermarket workers. Asda's recent production of *Black Friday* had exceptionally realistic fight scenes.) This open-access policy, however, does call into question Casting Networks' legitimacy as a professional directory. Their response was that by having no criteria that people had to meet, it eradicated the need for people to falsify credits in order to be accepted. That's a good point. I feel that actors buff up their credits on many occasions, for all sorts of reasons.

If you visit the Casting Networks page you will see that an awful lot of very well-respected English casting directors have given recommendations as to the effectiveness and their use of the system – a system that does seem to be tilted very much in their favour. I'm not sure that, for an unrepresented actor trying to apply for work on their own behalf, Casting Networks should be the first choice, but I do think it's worthwhile investigating.

Work Task

Check out Casting Networks online and take advantage of whatever free profile you are entitled to. As a represented actor, it should cost nothing and is just another toe that you're dipping in the pool. As an unrepresented actor, you will have to pay, and it might be a little frustrating as it may seem that nothing is happening as a result of your investment. It does mean that your picture and your CV, and your media if you choose to upload it, are available to the plethora of casting directors who are turning to Casting Networks.

***

There's absolutely no doubt that Spotlight is the big daddy of the casting services. It's also the brand that tells the world you are a professional actor, and it carries by far the most castings and information, and many of these are accessible to you if you don't have an agent. If you do have an agent you will see the information, but you won't be able to submit yourself and will have to get your agent to do that. Probably one of the reasons that Spotlight has become so innovative of late, is that it no longer has a monopoly in the market. Services like the others mentioned in this chapter, and the other free online services, all ensure that Spotlight has to work to keep ahead of the game. There are worries in some quarters that Spotlight chooses to carry unpaid work, something that the Equity job site refuses to do. As the market leader for 'professional' actors, Spotlight should perhaps rethink their policy on this. Do other trade journals carry unpaid work opportunities for trained professionals? I think not, and Spotlight perhaps might want to think about the fact that it's a premium brand and should carry premium opportunities. If actors do want to do unpaid work, there will be no shortage of websites happy to carry the information.

This isn't by any means a totally comprehensive look at casting sites, but it does look at the big players and see what they offer, so that you can make a decision about how useful they might be to you. It's worth checking out Shooting People, which is particularly good for short films, and Mandy.com, as well as having a look at Castweb, which is one of the older casting services. It doesn't send out briefs based on your filter, but rather emails you with a whole lot of casting opportunities every day, some of which you may be suitable for. Again, casting directors have a choice as to whether to circulate to all actors, or just to agents.

Work Task

Spend time online looking through the casting services available to you. You most probably won't be able to see the information they are offering without being a subscriber, or an existing member in the case of Equity and Spotlight, but the sites should offer you enough information, in addition to what you have just read, for you to be able to make a decision as to which site or sites might work for you.

- What do you want to get out of this casting service?

- Is it your only source of information?

- Would you like to use this casting service in conjunction with your existing Spotlight membership?

- If so, is it likely to give you information that Spotlight won't carry?

- What exactly do you get for your money?

There are other services such as Dramanic, The Page and Act On This, all of which may be worth a look. Apply the criteria you've read in this chapter to make a business assessment of their worth to you.

4. Making your showreel

It can be very hard to get screen work in the UK, even with an agent, so if you don't have an agent it is doubly difficult. Yet without screen work, what do you have to put on your showreel? And without a decent showreel, how are you going to get seen for screen work?

It's tricky. Many actors leave drama school without a showreel, a glaring omission in my opinion, as most young actors are more likely to be working for a few days on a television project during their first year than in the theatre – as borne out by the Drama UK research.

Having a showreel gives you an undeniable edge in getting into the room over someone who just submits a CV. It's also something that a casting director can and probably will keep on file. A good showreel doesn't have to be long. In fact, most casting directors readily admit that they find it difficult to watch something longer than four or five minutes. If they are good at their job, they will easily be able to make an assessment of your abilities and your suitability within that time. Two or three good clips can make a real difference. So you need to think about how to get them in order that your showreel doesn't consist of audition pieces shot against a blank wall, but shows you working on screen with viable production values that make you look good.

The low-budget film industry in the UK is considerable. Many films made on a shoestring go on to achieve greater acclaim, or a television showing. As fees on these can be low, quite often the information on casting is distributed to many sources and online casting services. The Spotlight casting service carries many of these, and the information is also circulated to agents. Sometimes agents may not look at these films due to the low fees available to their clients, and to get actors to appear in them, the producers have to do a considerable amount of chasing. Quite often the opportunities available in these films are something that actors may well wish to follow up themselves. Any suggestion made by you or your agent for film work should ideally be supported with a clip of your work on camera. This might be difficult. It's not only actors just starting out in their careers who have no showreel. I had nothing to show people for television work for the first ten years of my working life as an actor. This was in the days of video, but I couldn't afford a video machine or a camcorder. Then again, I didn't have any television work to record. It's a Catch-22 situation and it's not good. Agents often want to see something of you on camera when you write to them, particularly if you are not in a show in which they can come and see you work.

If you don't have any footage of yourself for a showreel, then one really accessible and rewarding avenue that should be followed up is that of the student film. There are an enormous number of benefits to be gained from an involvement in the student-film scene. The obvious one is that you're going to work with the next Steven Spielberg, who at this moment in time is currently studying in High Wycombe, and when he casts *Jaws XIV* he will remember you and that will be how you will break into Hollywood. Okay, so the odds of that happening are reasonably small, but you will be working with the directors, the producers, and the lighting cameramen of the future. The time you spend in the company of these people could be a very valuable investment.

Actors who are seeking agents are often very keen to throw themselves into fringe-theatre productions in order to get seen. A fringe-theatre production can involve several weeks of rehearsal, albeit scheduled around actors' availability at evenings and weekends, but rehearsing whole scenes with a character missing because they are doing a late shift at McDonald's can be a tad annoying. A fringe-theatre run can be as little as two weeks, depending on how much money the company has been able to stump up to pay the venue. If you're not particularly organised, and have not managed to get all your letters out to potential agents and casting directors in time, it can be very difficult to persuade them to come along at the last minute. They are busy, professional people and these visits are not pleasure – they have a limited amount of time and a limited number of visits of this nature that they can make. So you may very well get good reviews for your portrayal of Mike in a bitter and edgy new social comedy at the Kilburn Bikeshed, but once the run is over, that is it. The production exists no more, and if the agents that you want to impress didn't come along, then you're back at square one.

Student films will provide you with a copy of the film. These days they will give you a digital file that you can keep or edit and use as part of your showreel. This means that, for what could be a relatively short investment in terms of time, you could have something that can be sent out to agents or casting directors for several years.

Lots of student films are advertised on the casting services, but how do you work out just which ones are likely to give you a quality final product? The true answer is you can't be a hundred per cent certain, but basically, the more recognised and illustrious the course, the greater the likelihood of good resources and guidance for the students. Meet the students concerned. Many are so grateful to find actors that they will cast cold from a photo or a self-tape. Read the script. The mind of the film student can be a strange place. Ask what the payment terms are. Most offer expenses. Some offer a flat fee. Some film colleges have a standard agreement that they will ask you to sign. Remember that whatever you shoot will probably end up on YouTube in some form or another. Ask if you can keep the rights if the film is sold, so that you can then be paid according to the PACT agreement. They may or may not be in a position to agree to this, but it is worth asking.

I did a graduation film for someone at the National Film School. A story of witch-burning in the seventeenth century, it was filmed in a forest near Bishop Stortford over ten days. We were all paid ten pounds per day. Having one of the lead roles, I asked to sign an agreement that if the film were sold, I would receive the minimum payment that my performance would pay in those circumstances. The film was a great success and looked good. It was a good addition to what at that time was a very slim showreel. Three years later, an envelope dropped onto my doormat with a cheque for a couple of thousand pounds. The film had been sold to BBC Two schools television, and had been shown three times. Great for the director, and not bad for me either.

★★★

Maryisia Trembecka is an actress who came into the profession after working as a trader in financial institutions. As with anyone coming into the business later, making one's mark can be even harder. In order to get good material on her showreel and generate more work, Marysia seized with both hands the opportunities presented by a short film. Here's what she has to say on the subject.

How do you get this sort of work?

Casting Call Pro has lots of unpaid film work, far more than Spotlight. Mandy.com is something I don't use often, but I have booked two films that way. Also through being recommended by other directors, I recently did a film noir for a director with whom I had previously played Mrs Santa Claus and who was now assisting another student director.

What are the benefits of doing short films?

Some benefits are obvious: you *may* get useable footage for your showreel, and you may get networking opportunities. More importantly you are getting to practise the art of acting. It is always easier to get more acting work when you are busy making films and easier to answer that dreaded casting question: 'So what have you been up to?' You get live practice of being relaxed and honest on camera and not being too 'theatrical' – I watched some people auditioning the other day for a film role and you could see those who have done a lot of theatre and not much screen work. Watching the crew do their job, you really understand where you, as an actor, fit in. You are there to move the story along. You understand why listening and reacting is so important in film, as it gives the filmmaker options, and you begin to see how you can be left on the cutting-room floor for the sake of the story. There is more freedom to play with characters, costume, make-up, than on television and in big-budget productions. You can have a lot more creative input and you have the chance to play better, larger, different roles than you might in bigger budget movies.

What are the downsides to this sort of work?

The downsides tend to centre around people's inexperience. Though some students are very mature, first-time or student directors, producers, writers, directors of photography, are still learning themselves – and a disorganised shoot is often an unhappy one. I have had to argue hard to get travel expenses repaid, even though they had been pre-approved, and had to threaten to contact film schools as I could not get the finished film or any stills. I have slept in a hallway with my fellow actress on a mattress, been starved, travelled hundreds of miles to find that my main co-star has cancelled, so I only shot two minutes of film and had to do the same journey all over again for a further minute. The worst was a sulky costume and make-up girl having tantrums on set (I thought that was the actress's prerogative!), and most of the crew drinking alcohol for my scene mid-takes.

What's the best experience you have had doing short films?

My best experience was doing a Kickstarter-funded short called *Shudder*. The entire crew were very experienced. It was a huge, brilliantly organised shoot about war photographers. I acted on green screen for the first time, and got that Bruce Willis moment of walking nonchalantly through bullets and explosions whilst covered in dirt and then pulling shrapnel out of myself. I have the most incredible production stills and the director, who has done VFX on films such as the *Harry Potter* series, is now painstakingly making his film frame by frame. It would not surprise me if it wins a few festival awards.

Do people think that's all you do?

I don't put all these credits on my CV and Spotlight. Some I use only for a production still, a clip or the experience. I now cherry-pick any low-budget work.

Has the student-film work led to more mainstream opportunities?

As a result of the networking involved I have occasionally been called in for castings. I now have a much better showreel of me playing everything from Victorian ladies to murderers. I have had castings and immediate bookings as a result of my showreel, much of which is low-budget and student material.

Work Task

Search the internet and find details for the top film courses for student directors. The National School of Film and Television, Bournemouth Film School and the University of the Creative Arts in Farnham will probably figure on it.

- Email them and find out who is the head of the film course and who is responsible for casting student films.

- Do they have a database of actors that students can call on when casting their graduation films?

- If not, how are they cast? Who should you be writing to?

Note this in your work plan.

Search out short-film competitions online. How do they source their actors?

Does your agent know that you would be happy to do this type of work? Agents tend not to chase this type of work as it doesn't have any financial reward. Have a chat with your agent and be clear about why you feel it would be good to do something along these lines.

5. Building your website

These days, everybody has a website. You know that from your own personal life. Want to book a holiday? You look for the travel company's website. Looking for a good handyman near you? You start by looking at their website. Theatres have websites, and for most, it's now the first point of contact with their audience. An information and booking portal, a theatre's website is vital in creating the relationship that will bring people through its doors. Television programmes have websites, and undoubtedly television actors have websites. Quite often the website of the solo performer, or television personality, will be managed by fans, or their agency.

So what of you, the Working Actor, and your need to have a digital presence? Is it a worthwhile and necessary tool in the armoury of the twenty-first-century actor looking for work? Or is it enough that you have a page in Spotlight, or on one of the casting services that a potential employer can be directed to?

To make employers aware of us in the past, we used to send out hard copies of our CVs, which were probably accompanied by 10'x8" photographs, which cost you money every time you made a submission for work. Now most of those CVs and photographs are submitted digitally. Ideally, every CV that is submitted should be tailored to that particular job. Reorder your credits, putting the most relevant ones at the top. The world of cut-and-paste should mean there is no excuse for a one-size-fits-all CV being sent out.

There is, though, a great need for you to have control over your online presence. Your own website gives you an opportunity to select the best material that you have available, and that shows you in a good light. When you're chasing a job opportunity, or about to go to meet a director, the first thing you should do is check them out online. When people are going to meet you, some of them may do exactly the same thing. A website gives you a first-class opportunity to present your information in the way that you want it to be seen. You might want to upload headshots, your showreel, information about what you've been up to, reviews, a biography, television or theatre work that you've taken part in. There are lots of companies who design and provide websites at a reasonable cost, but these days it's relatively easy to set up your own. Free website builders such as www.wix.com and www.weebly.com provide templates and tutorials that can get a pretty smart-looking, basic page up there within an hour or so's work.

Your name is your brand and as such you should own it, and that means owning your name in digital terms. With the ongoing release of more and more domain names, it should be relatively easy to be able to find your name with a suffix that is still available. Unless, of course, you're Benedict Cumberbatch or Matt Smith. (And if you are, why are you reading this?)

There is a saying that clever people know lots of things, but successful people know lots of people. Getting your name out there is all part of the necessary networking process. It allows people to get to know you. Lots of people spend time browsing the internet, and may just come across you by chance. Your URL should be printed on any business cards you have. The web is probably the world's biggest shop window. Plumbers, international charities, huge entertainment corporations and governments all know its worth. You need to as well.

A final thought that I came across in an article on the web about actors and their websites. 'Have a look at my website' might be just the response you are looking for when people say to you: 'Oh, you're an actor, are you? So what have you been in?' It might also be something that proud mums and dads can look at and point inquisitive relatives to when times are not at their best.

You can also link your website to your Twitter account if you have one. It's hard to define where the personal ends and the professional begins, and nowhere is it more blurred than in the world of social media. It's well documented that employers do research people on the internet before job appointments. I'm not sure that this applies to actors as much as it might do to other professions, but it's certainly worth thinking about. You can make your Facebook profile accessible only to your friends, and you might think about using it to be the more personal aspect of your social-media presence. Twitter can be used to get your thoughts and information out into the world. (More on this later.)

A good, professional-looking website with the right information, a good selection of photos and video clips, and links to social-media streams, can be an invaluable marketing tool for any actor. It may be a financial investment, but it's one that you should think seriously about making.

Work Task

Get onto the internet and see if the domain name that you want to buy is available. Register your domain.

Try out one of the free website production services. You can build a basic website on these sites at little or no cost. You should then be able to manage your domain name with the host company so that it points at your free website. There may be an upgrade charge to do this with some of the free sites, but the advantage is that this means that people searching for your website or putting your name into a search engine should end up on your page.

Upload at least one recent headshot, your ten best credits with the most recent first, a few statistics regarding height, etc. and colouring if the photograph is black-and-white, and some contact details. Be very careful what contact details you put up onto the web. Websites are scanned for email addresses regularly, and this may produce a lot of spam suddenly arriving in your inbox. Use an online contacts form on your site for people to get in contact with you. Make sure that your home address is not displayed in any way on your site. Websites are scanned by lots of people, and this may produce some strange people wearing not a lot of natural fibre on your doorstep. Especially if you've ever appeared in *Doctor Who*!

Publish the website. Services such as Wix will be able to sort out such things as SEO, or 'search-engine optimisation'. This means getting your website as far up the listings as possible so that, when your name is searched for, the link to your website is one of the first things displayed. It's worth thinking about how many people will randomly be looking for your website. If you will be including the URL of your site in emails and letters to casting directors and/or agents, then it might not be worth the extra expenditure at this point. If you do feel that people will be searching for you on the internet, and you want them to find the site quickly, then SEO is a necessity.

By the end of a couple of hours' work, you can have an up-to-date, easily changeable, and exceptionally accessible website available to the entire world at very little cost.

6. Writing a winning letter

In the redbrick Yorkshire grammar school that I attended during the 1970s, we learned many things. Much of that knowledge I have had no reason to use over the last forty years, but some has stood me in good stead. Mr JB Gunn was the English master responsible for teaching me how to write a business letter. Use of the correct layout and the appropriate terminology is something that I have held onto until this day. When I started out as an actor, one of my most prized possessions was a state-of-the-art portable typewriter, bought as a Christmas present by my parents, which managed to escape two burglaries in my student accommodation. At least once a week I would settle down at my dining table in my bedsit, a well-thumbed copy of *Contacts* by my side, and, armed with carbon paper and Tippex, I would write letters to theatres. I was very proud of those letters, typed on the best quality paper I could afford, and sent, along with a photograph, to repertory theatres from Sunderland to Stoke, and from Yeovil to York.

The letters obviously brought results as I spent the first four years of my career moving from rep to rep without an agent, and the theatres phoned me direct to arrange auditions. So the phrase: 'We'll keep your letter on file until something comes up' was not just an idle threat in those days. They actually did it. These days it might be harder to believe that they still do file communications direct from actors, particularly given the move from paper to email. Easier to delete, no hassle of storage.

Given that even rep theatres these days often employ casting directors, there might be no guarantee that your letter in a theatre filing cabinet will ever be looked at. Yet there is always the chance, and chance is what you as an actor have to survive on. Or luck, as some people may call it.

Do not undervalue the effectiveness of a letter. Good hard copy which can serve as an introduction. Look at creating a CV which has a photograph within it and can be printed on good-quality notepaper to accompany the letter, which saves you the added cost of hard photograph envelopes, and also extra postage.

The use of email has also brought about an informality. When I first began using email some fourteen years ago, I assumed that every time I sat down and clicked on new message, that I was writing a letter. True, I didn't have to fill in all the address details. Ah, how well I remember Mr JB Gunn's instructions. My address and details in the top right-hand corner of the paper aligned to the right-hand side, and then, if a business letter, the addressee's details aligned to the left-hand side. Then a suitable space followed by the appropriate salutation 'Dear (insert name here)'. I would always sign off an email with 'Yours sincerely' just as if I was writing a letter. I've found that it's been very useful to try and maintain this level of formality for all my business emails ever since. Occasionally I slip up. I just type in a quick reply and send it, and it never looks good. I know that, because I receive a lot of emails which are exactly the same. Sentences that were meant to be spoken appear typed in front of me. At best they come across as chatty and incoherent, and at worst they come across as brusque and abrupt. So maintaining the letter format, and the discipline contained therein, can help to give emails a useful and clarifying formality. Once you have received a reply, you can let that dictate the style in which you continue the conversation.

Some people I know do still compose a letter, laying it out correctly on the paper, and then turning the letter into a PDF document so that the formatting is retained, and attaching it to an email. It does mean that you then have to write a note in the email as to what the letter is about. Remember, though, that not many people will open unsolicited emails with an attachment. You can paste the PDF into the email so that it is easily visible. A good business-letter layout will always impress, and it does allow you to file away the document for your reference. It is probably important to remember that not everybody has Microsoft Word on their computer. Some of us have made the Damascene conversion to the world of Mac, so send your letter, and indeed your CV, as a PDF document, so that when it's opened on another machine the formatting will be retained, and all your careful work will not be lost.

The best letter has a reason for being written. As someone who casts corporate videos and role-play jobs, I've had lots of general letters and unsolicited emails sent to me saying something along the lines of: 'I'm looking to do some corporate work and I'd be really grateful if you would bear me in mind when something comes up.'

The problem with this is that the request is incredibly unspecific, and so all the work involved in fulfilling it is on my side. I have to file the letter or the email. I have to keep you in mind. I have to try and think of what you would be suitable for, even though I didn't ask you to write to me. The best letter has a specific request which is easy to answer. For example, if you're writing to me for corporate role-play work, then your first letter may be a simple one asking: 'How do you source the actors you use for your role-play work?'

It would be rude of me not to drop you a quick line and tell you. I may not be able to write positively saying that I source actors through unsolicited emails, but I will at least be able to give you some information that you can act on. I may say that I source people on a job-by-job basis, or from personal recommendation, both of which should give you a lead to either reply to me saying 'When would be the best time to drop you my CV and photograph?' or to find someone who knows me and who can recommend your work to me.

The casting director Hannah Miller commented:

> 'It's really important to remember it's a professional contact, so write the email as you would a letter, but it has to be brief and to the point... I was given some very good advice a long time ago, that applies to almost any covering letter and CV – the letter is like a trailer for the CV. So it's a taster. You want to make the reader turn over and look at the photo and the CV rather than just, in prose form, write everything that's on your CV.'

Similarly, writing to a casting director and asking if they would 'bear you in mind' is probably not going to yield results. You need to have something to show them, or something to ask them. Asking them how you can get ten minutes of their time over a cup of coffee might be a much more positive way forward than asking if they will keep your details in mind for anything they have coming up. If you have done your research properly, you should know what they have coming up. Getting in to see them is what's important. No one is going to cast you from a piece of paper and a photograph.

A letter to an agent asking for representation is also one that makes it very easy for them to send a negative reply to you very quickly. The letter that asks if you might be able to come in and say hello is one that is much more likely to produce results.

So any letter or email you send needs to have a specific point to it, something that is easily achievable by both parties, and something that is not unreasonable. Unsolicited letters asking for work often are. Targeting your letters and emails is also key. On a good afternoon way back in 1978, with my trusty typewriter at my fingertips, I could probably manage five or six letters. My typing is still pretty poor, but these days I have the luxury of being able to dictate whatever I'm writing to my computer. If you ever had an email from me, then you may have experienced just how effective my dictation software is. It's quick Brillo Pad! (Most of the time it works.) The point is that all of those five or six letters would be individual letters. The graduate who, with great pride, says that they have just sent out fifty letters to casting directors may actually mean that they just sent out the same word-processed letter to fifty casting directors. Some people use even less effort and send a BCC'd email. That's not asking for work, that's sending junk mail.

A good, effective letter has to be written in such a way that it could only be sent to the person to whom it is addressed. Why are you writing to that particular person? What point of reference do you have that is unique to them? Don't go over the top with unfeeling praise about their latest exploits (unless, of course, you're a real fan of whatever it is they have been working on and that is why you're writing – but then that's a fan letter, and not a professional enquiry about work). Keep the letter to one page, well laid out and with a one-page CV, preferably with a small photograph attached or even better as part of the CV itself. If you're sending this as an email, then please check the size of the photograph file. While internet connections are much better than they have been in the past, it can still be incredibly frustrating when checking one's email on a portable device, to suddenly find you are trying to download a large file. Learn how to compress pictures.

In talking about effective letters and emails, I might just mention some things that I have experienced in the past, just to be sure. Please check that you have spelt the name of your recipient correctly, and more importantly that of the company they work for. In the past I have been: 'Dear Sir', 'Dear Paul Claydon', 'Dear Mr Claton', 'Dear Director', and, this is without a word of a lie, 'Dear person who is directing *Privates on Parade* at Greenwich this Christmas'. Mercifully none of them chose to write 'Dear Dad', which would have got an immediate response.

Remember that any email sent is part of a professional relationship, so if you're suffering from insomnia, don't be tempted to fire off lots of emails at 2:14 a.m. Write them during the night by all means, but then save them in your draft folder or use a 'send later' programme and send them during business hours. There is no guaranteed time to receive unsolicited mail, but I can suggest that any emails you send on a Monday morning will get ignored. Come to that, Friday afternoon isn't great either!

Think of when your own downtime is. Perhaps late afternoon and towards the end of the week. Not around 5:30 p.m. when the person concerned is trying to meet an end-of-working-day deadline, but mid-afternoon when there might be a lull. That's the time to check the email one last time and hit 'send'. No guarantee, but it can't hurt yout chances.

The key elements of the successful letter, be it to a casting director, venue, director or agent are:

- Who are you?

- What can you do?

- What are you asking for?

Keep it as short as you can. Be polite. Be direct. Be honest.

Work Task

Select three people to whom you're going to write a letter in the next five days. Note down what you're asking for, the reason you're writing, and why you are writing specifically to them.

Write the three letters and file them away in your Working Actor file. Send one as a hard copy, send one as a PDF attachment and send one as an email formatted as a letter.

You could ask a trusted friend or colleague to look over the letter before you send it, or write it and leave it a while before sending it. Sometimes coming back to something afresh can inspire you that little bit more. I'm sure Mr JB Gunn would have approved of that.

Keep a record of letters sent and a list of to whom you have written. See what the results are.

7. Coping with rejection

'Actors search for rejection. If they don't get it, they reject themselves.'

Charlie Chaplin

You don't need me to tell you that, as an actor, you will have to face an awful lot of disappointment. You won't have been out of drama school long before you realise that. It might even have started during the drama-school application process when you might have been turned down from schools you auditioned for, possibly even your first-choice school. If that was the case, and you have now completed your training at another establishment, you have learned the first lesson. You've got on with it. You have made it work. That's what it's all about. As one door closes, another one opens... somewhere! It may not be immediately apparent where the new opportunity is, but it will be there somewhere, waiting for you. Finding it is the challenge.

Marianne O'Connor trained as an actress. She did well throughout her twenties, but not well enough that, when motherhood called, she felt that she could rely on acting as a sole source of income. She had a very successful career as an actor in the corporate world, and she set about gaining herself some business-coaching qualifications. Now she works all over Europe as a business coach, one to one with senior executives, working on skills and qualities they need in their working lives. Gravitas, negotiating skills, and resilience. That last quality, the essential ability to bounce back, seemed to me to be something that actors need by the bucketful. I asked Marianne for some thoughts on how one becomes more resilient:

'One of the hardest parts of being an actor is the constant rejection, and one of the most vital is your ability to deal with that rejection.'

The reality of the industry is that the rejection usually has very little to do with talent and is more often based on something you can't control. You were too tall, or just the wrong look – nothing that you could know or do anything about. That doesn't help when you get rejected. The trick is how you view those experiences and more importantly *what* you do with them. Marianne pointed out that the ability to flex your thinking, manage your emotions and adjust your actions in challenging situations, is governed by your overall resilience. It is your flexibility that enables you to remain self-aware and responsive in times of stress. Some of the most successful actors cite their setbacks and failures as their most formative experiences; experiences that have moved them forward and propelled them to success. I asked if she thought that the more resilient we were, the easier our life as an actor would be:

'Resilience does not eliminate stress or erase problems. Instead it gives you the strength to tackle problems head on, overcome adversity and move on with your life. Your ability to manage your emotions in high-stake situations can have a huge impact in terms of how you are perceived by others. People who are able to keep their cool under pressure have what psychologists call resilience.'

So how can you, as a Working Actor, become more resilient?

Build positive beliefs in your abilities: Remind yourself of your strengths, accomplishments and successes. Actors tend to be their own harshest critic, so focus on what you do well and leverage those qualities by playing to your strengths. Resilient individuals tend to believe that the actions they take directly affect the outcome of an event. This 'outcome frame' thinking significantly impacts on your ability to focus on what you want versus what is getting in the way. Remember that there are factors you cannot influence – your height, build, etc. – so focus on the ones you have in your control.

Find a sense of purpose: Learn from each experience. Get into the habit of asking for feedback and raise your levels of self-awareness. One of the characteristics of resilience is the understanding that life is full of challenges. How we react to those challenges is what makes the difference.

Develop a strong support network: Everybody needs friends – people you were at drama school with, people you have worked with, or using places such as the Actors Centre to come into contact with other working professionals. American actors are particularly good at this. They understand the value of this 'emotional currency' and focus their energy by taking classes to build confidence and develop their network. They understand the importance of defining a strong personal brand to build their profile and visibility in the industry.

Embrace change: Flexibility is an essential part of resilience, and this is something most actors excel at. I recently sat in on an audition for actors who were looking to supplement their income by working in the corporate-training sector. I was hugely impressed by their understanding of the 'business' of acting. They all demonstrated an ability to utilise other skill sets and multitask in the pursuit of their acting career. Often you may find a way forward in your career by using your skills in something that was not part of your training. For some, this can bring a fulfilment that allows them to move into this area full time.

Be outcome focused: Articulate SMART career goals that are Specific, Measurable, Achievable, Realistic and Time-bound. This will enable you to proactively plan your future. (We will look at this in detail in the next chapter.)

Don't give up: Research has shown that resilience is not an extraordinary thing. It is something that can be acquired. In terms of success it can be 'the difference that makes the difference'.

Work Task

Think of a recent rejection, something that did not turn out the way you would have liked.

Note down all the positive things that you felt you did as part of that process. Interview technique, engaging the interviewer, the qualities or credits that got you the interview.

Note down the feedback that you would give yourself. Try to steer this away from just 'Get the job next time!' and make it as specific as possible. How engaging were you in the interview? What did you talk about that was relevant to the job? Did you make the meeting work? (More ideas on this later in the book.)

Write down how you might change these constructive points into action in your next interview or meeting.

This process can turn an unproductive experience or interview into something from which you can acquire and develop the resilience that you need to keep moving forward in your working life.

8. Measuring success

As an actor you are a business. You are CEO, chief financial officer, marketing manager, head of operations and tea boy in the business of you (actually, if you have an understanding partner you might not have to fulfil the role of tea boy), but all other posts will have to be things in which you are skilled. It's easy to realise that an actor has to be a good administrator – organising appointments, keeping receipts, sorting scripts and the like – but hopefully you will start to see just how important it is to adopt the other roles that any successful business has.

If you were part of a team running a successful business, you would have colleagues and associates who would be a daily part of your working life. You would have an office to go to each day, and you would have a way of measuring how successful you are – sales targets, appraisals, key performance indicators. Hopefully you do have a place that you associate with work, be it just a desk in a room or a study at home where you can be 'at work'. You probably have friends and acquaintances who are in a similar position to you, and may be able to offer advice when needed and help you see both sides of any situation. You are almost certainly a member of a professional body, such as Spotlight or Equity, where professional advice is available should you need it. But just how do you measure success? How do you know how well you're doing?

Earlier this year, I spent an hour with the final year graduating students at ALRA, a drama school. The principal there introduced me to a sea of expectant faces late on a Thursday afternoon. Whenever I stand or sit in front of a new group of people, I always feel that they are surveying me with those wary, cagey eyes of youth as if to say: 'Why you?'

I asked about their dreams. They certainly had them. I asked what practical preparations they were making to become Working Actors. Some had thought about that too. I asked how they would know when it was time to give up! Perhaps that wasn't a question they were expecting, but the answers ranged from: 'When I don't like it any more,' to 'When the passion dies.'

I then moved on to ask that if I came back to see them again in a year's time, how would they know if they had been successful?

The answers were a little vague. Some of them knew they wanted to do some theatre, and some thought they might work in television, but none of them had any objectives.

This is where treating your career as a commercial concern can be a great help. You are the manager of your business. You are also the team who make the operation work. In the business world, managers who are responsible for whole teams of people know that it's very important that they give their teams objectives. Not only objectives, but objectives that are measurable and can be looked at and reviewed. These are known as SMART objectives, and are common in many businesses.

Having set SMART objectives, it means that a manager can review an employee's performance in a year's time and understand how to measure it. A SMART objective is as follows:

Specific: For you as an actor this would mean not simply saying: 'I want to do some telly.' It would mean saying: 'I want to do at least two days' television work.'

Measurable: Any objective that you set has to have some way of being measured. So, in setting an objective for yourself as an actor, how would you measure the objective? Would you measure it in terms of number of days worked? Would you measure it in terms of amount of money earned? Measuring it in terms of 'it's something that might get me noticed' is a little harder. How do you assess that? One of the key points of setting a SMART objective is that you will have a definite scale of measurement to judge it by.

Achievable: It's understable to dream of playing the lead in a major Hollywood blockbuster in your first year out of drama school, but in reality you won't. It's great to have dreams, but here we are talking about practical, achievable objectives. If a major film role is your objective and will serve as a measure of your success, then you're setting yourself up to fail. Put the major Hollywood blockbuster on your dreams list, and set yourself a target that looks achievable: a day's television work; a fringe run in London; something you know might come along. This is not lowering your sights, it's looking at your career in a realistic and businesslike way, so that at the end of the year you will have a chance of fulfilling your objectives and have a feeling of success.

Relevant: It's not much help just saying that you want to do ten days' work so that, at the end of the year, you can count any number of days spent on the till at Lidl in your work total. The work has to be based on your skill set as an actor. For example, if one of your objectives is financial ('I would like to earn five thousand pounds from acting work') then theatre, television, corporate, or promotional earnings can all be counted towards that target.

Timed: Give yourself a specific time frame for the objective. One year from the day you left drama school, one calendar year, one year from the day you start this business plan. Whatever it may be, let it be a period of time that you can measure easily.

★★★

Objectives such as these are the beginning of a business plan which any good business needs in order to succeed. And, as I have said, as an actor, that's what you are... a business.

So give your business every chance of success.

Work Task

Start a set of SMART objectives for yourself.

Write down three objectives that you'd like to achieve during the next year.

Next to each objective, write down the five SMART criteria – why they are specific, measurable, achievable, relevant and timed – and ensure that your objectives fulfil them.

9. Overcoming your mistakes

Auditions and interviews are opportunities. They are the link between the world of work and the world of being an actor who is looking for work. Every actor will have their own nightmare story about auditions and so will you – unless, as yet, you haven't been to many. People say that it's always worth going along to an audition just for the experience, and yet not all experiences are positive. Mark Rylance told me how he almost turned back on the way to his first audition for the RSC, and then when he went into the room, he did his *Hamlet* speech in Japanese! It was sufficiently interesting for the director to ask him to work on it again... in English.

There are many instances of a high level of humiliation and sense of failure involved with the audition process. You, the Working Actor, have to ride this out to get work. Each time the audition doesn't work in your favour, you have to get back on the horse and try again. Even now, I approach some auditions with a sense of dread, and not always on my own part. You will meet directors and casting directors who don't know what they're doing. You will be asked to do stupid things. You will be asked to mime (particularly difficult for me as I was absent on the afternoon when my drama school did mime) and show the difference between hard and soft toilet paper. You will be asked lots of stupid questions, and yet, from all these experiences, you will grow.

Given that we are all prone to these mishaps, there is a certain sense of Schadenfreude in reading those of others, knowing that we are a just a step away from such trials. So let's indulge ourselves a little in the misfortunes and tribulations of others, but above all, let's look at what we might learn from their mistakes.

- 'Not checking where the location actually is! And not reading the whole script and so not realising the slimy solicitor with the wife and kids was actually gay!!' – Always double-check where you are going. Turning up late is an absolute no-no. Make sure you are fully prepared. Read the whole script if you have been sent it.

- 'I did my genuine native Yorkshire accent for a bread commercial once and the director asked me why I was talking funny.' – Be prepared for all opinions of your work. They are not necessarily right, but they have the right to have them.

- 'Took all three kids to an audition in Manchester, thought it would be fairly easy by car. Got stuck on M6. All three children car sick. Everywhere. Luckily I left with bags of time and changes of clothes. Just got there on time, slightly smelling of vomit. Narrowly missed receiving parking ticket. Got recall, went by train. (Didn't get job though.)' – Don't make things harder for yourself than they need to be.

Managing your life as well as your work is all part of the job. If you feel at your best, you will do better.

My grateful thanks to all the actors who submitted stories, and I'm sure you will have many of your own. Here are my three favourites:

- 'Once freaked out a television director because I had done a lot of googling, found out loads about him and slowly came across as a bit of a stalker. Didn't get that job – and expected to get a restraining order in the post for days afterwards.'

- 'When asked to "make love to a chair" in an audition I picked it up and smashed it into the wall, turned round and said: "There you go, it's fucked." Wasn't what they had in mind, apparently!'

- 'I auditioned for a director years ago – I did my two songs and I thought it went quite well. I said my goodbyes and left. Unfortunately, I went out the wrong door and found myself standing in a broom cupboard. As I stood there wondering what to do I heard the next person come in and begin his audition. I stood in the cupboard listening to them sing and thinking, "How the hell can I get out of this now?" – the next guy finished and, as he was leaving, the director shouted, "It's the second door on the right, not the first, that's a cupboard... you can come out of the closet now!" How everyone laughed... Needless to say I didn't get the job. So rule number eleven – know where the exit is.'

While editing this book I went for a casting myself at BBC Elstree for a daytime drama. I had a great meeting, lots of easy-flowing conversation between myself and two casting directors, the director and producer. The reading went well and I walked out of the room on a high, only to realise moments later that my bag was still on the floor of the room by the chair. A big deep breath, and I headed back in with the pronouncement: 'Don't worry, I'm not here to see you again. It's just that my antidepression tablets are in my bag and I left it in here.' I headed out of the room thinking: 'Why? Why did you say that?' I didn't get the job.

So, what can you learn from the audition process and its associated nightmares? My perception of auditions changed enormously once I began to sit on the other side of the table. From 1984 until 2010 I auditioned young people for the National Youth Theatre every year, and from 1990, when I started my theatre directing career, and I began to appreciate just how actors come over in interviews. The ones who are so desperate for the job that you don't see any real personality. The one whose ability is entirely muddied by nerves, and the occasional relief of the person who seems in control, and who as a result makes you feel at ease also.

It's always good to remember that the people meeting you want you to be right. They aren't looking for wrong people, they are on your side. When I sit on an audition panel, I'm nervous too, and it is a great strain meeting new people all day and being nice to them. People who make me feel relaxed are a real joy to see.

Let's face it, auditions don't ever become something you can sail through. They will always demand nervous energy, preparation, and thought. It might seem that they get easier just by having done so many of them, but in reality, at each and every interview, you can be at the mercy of the people you're meeting. So let's look in the next chapter at how you can make the meeting work!

Work Task

I think the best way of getting an understanding of the audition process is to sit on the other side of the table. See how nervous you feel, and how easily embarrassed as you cope with the nerves and fears of the audition-ees. You may know a director who is working on a fringe show, or your old drama school may be doing auditions and may want a graduate on the panel. Volunteer as an usher, or if needed, offer to read in. Watching people in the audition situation when the pressure is off you can be quite revelatory. Watch their eye contact. Note their questions. Would you give them the job?

Have you ever had any feedback on how you come across in auditions? Perhaps it might be worth investigating an audition-technique workshop, just to concentrate purely on how you were perceived in the audition situation. Many workshops use video feedback, which can be exceptionally useful in examining just how you are coming across to people. If you haven't had an audition in a while, doing a dry run for someone can be very, very helpful. It can get you back to being match fit.

10. Making meetings work

So, you have got the meeting, interview or audition. Well done. Your agent has sent you an email telling you where and when, and attached to it are a couple of sides of script that you're going to read. How are you going to make the best of this opportunity – in the ten or fifteen minutes you get with someone who has the capacity to give you the job?

Most people in their working lives have few job interviews. My partner has reached the dizzy heights of a major company and has only had two job interviews in nearly twenty years of work. It's not unknown for some actors to have two interviews per week, for that is what each and every audition is – it's a job interview. It's an easy thing to forget. If you have spent a few weeks, or a few months, languishing out of work, the appointed time in your diary can seem like the light at the end of the tunnel. For some, however, it is the headlight of an oncoming train, rushing towards you, and the nerves associated with this meeting can prevent you from functioning at your best. So just how do you make the meeting work? Any successful meeting can be divided into six stages, which cover before, during and afterwards.

They are:

- Preparation.

- First impressions.

- Building rapport.

- 'What have you been up to recently?'

- The escape.

- Following up.

Let's take a look at each of those six stages in turn and what exactly you can do to make them work in your favour.

Preparation

Preparation is ultimately the key to success. 'Fail to prepare and prepare to fail' is as true for the audition situation as it is for the military campaign. Plan everything, from knowing your travel arrangements and checking that the shirt you think is the right one to wear has been ironed, to double-checking the location of the meeting online or on a map. All this is part of the regime that will get you stepping into the room in the right frame of mind.

Very few auditions or meetings now require you to do an audition speech. Perhaps if you're going for a general casting at a theatre, you may be asked to take along a couple of speeches, and sometimes fringe-theatre shows who are seeing a lot of people ask you to bring an audition speech for a first audition. Sometimes the first-round audition for a season at the RSC can demand a speech. Or they may ask you to prepare something they have sent through. Whatever the case, you wouldn't dream of turning up without knowing your speech. You had it drummed into you at drama school. Yet people who have been sent a couple of pages of script in an email by their agent, or by a casting director in preparation for an interview, often turn up with a less than comprehensive knowledge of the text. Learn the script. It doesn't matter if you stumble on it in the interview. It's not a memory test, but it shows that you have made an effort, and it makes it considerably easier for the director or the casting director to assess your suitability for the role if your head isn't buried in a piece of paper with your eyes looking downwards.

In the real world, most job interviews are designed to assess both suitability and competence. As actors we are lucky in that, on many occasions, competence has already been assessed by the time we step through the door. Your agent assessed your competence before taking you on. The casting director has seen a showreel, or knows your work, or trusts your agent's recommendations. So the main point of this interview will be to assess your suitability for the role in question. However, anyone might come to doubt your competence when the first thing they see is that you seem to have an inability to learn the words.

Scripts can arrive late. Most castings in the world of television these days seem to be organised at 4 p.m. on the day before they want to see you. Make time to learn the script, or at least to be so familiar with it that you don't need to keep your eyes looking down at it throughout the reading. If your sight-reading isn't good, then mark this down as one of the things you might want to work on during your next period of unemployment. Pick up a newspaper each day and record yourself reading a paragraph out loud. Listen back to it. Constant practice will really make a difference. If it's a commercial casting and no script has been sent, then make it part of your preparation to arrive for the interview a good twenty minutes early in order to look at the script and prepare it. The scripts are nearly always waiting on arrival, and if you're not sure, check with your agent beforehand.

Plan your travel. There is a law as yet unwritten, but probably called the 'Southern Trains Law', that dictates public transport will do everything in its power to delay you. Much better to plan to get there early and loiter in one of the plethora of coffee emporia that are bound to be on a street near your meeting.

There is an awful lot of debate over how to dress for interviews and auditions. In some cases, particularly for commercials, the dress might be dictated. Only last week I went up for a commercial in which I was a prospective butler. The instructions were extraordinarily specific: white shirt, black tie, and suit or dark jacket. Some actors had decided to put their own spin on this. One had gone so far as to make it a bow tie and a pair of pink sequinned shoes. I'm not sure that did him any favours, but when I opened the door to the casting suite, yes there were a whole – what is the correct collective noun? – a whole sneer of butlers. It doesn't help make you feel individual, or wanted, but if that is what has been asked for, then wear it. If no direction has been given, then I always feel it's better to err on the smart side. After all, this is a job interview, and in the real world most people would go to a job interview looking good.

First impressions

'You don't get a second chance to make a first impression.' It may be a rather banal observation but it is true. The casting director has looked at your photograph and read your CV. They may know your work and they may have met you before. The director likewise. There is a school of thought that says, until you open the door and come into the room, you've probably got the job! Unless you have been brought in as a 'pushing the envelope here' idea by the casting director, the reason you got the appointment is that you are suitable for the role and competent to play it. So how do you stop things changing the moment you enter the room?

I know the occasions I've been disappointed when an actor has walked in the room have been mainly because their headshot hasn't been a true representation of the person, or because it would take an awful lot of work from the current state they are in to make them actually look like the photograph.

You need to go into the room looking recognisably like your headshot. This is what has got you here, and if you're greeted by a look of surprise, then you need to think about changing either your headshot or appearance. Recently we held the second round of the Alan Bates Award at the Actors Centre. The photographs of the twenty finalists were laid out so that we, the judges, could identify them as they worked. All seemed good, except we couldn't find one smiling, floppy, blond-haired boy in the room. There was a tall man with a ginger beard and a shaven head who would have been a shoo-in for any castings about historic rebellions. Trying to convince myself that he wasn't someone who had just wandered in off the street, I looked at the photo again but there seemed to be very little similarity and so at the break we asked him: 'Is this your photograph?'

'Yes,' he replied. He seemed remarkably unalarmed. Taking the bull by the horns is one of my specialities: it doesn't always work but on this occasion I felt it was called for. 'Then you need to change it,' I said. 'This is what has got you in the room, and this is what people are expecting to see. The look you have today is great... slightly aggressive, but great. But if that's the look you're selling, then you need to have photographs that show it.'

A realisation dawned over him, and he saw what we were saying. 'I thought it just gave them two different looks to work with, but I see what you mean.'

He got some new photos done and they look great, and that shaven-headed, ginger-bearded, peasant look may well just work.

You may be announced into the room by a busy assistant who is showing people in, or the casting director themselves may have come to collect you. Either way, as you step into the room try to take the initiative. Say 'hello' as you enter, rather than as you cross the room and get to the people sitting down. Part of the mystery of auditions and interviews is that you never know what, or sometimes who, is behind the door. Television meetings are often conducted in quite small interview rooms, while theatre meetings can be held anywhere from the stage-management office to the actual stage. As a very young actor in my first year of work, I once went for an audition at the Old Vic. Having been kept waiting for twenty minutes in a small, poky dressing

room with three other actors, I was collected by someone and shown along a corridor. They opened the door
at the end of the corridor and, stepping through it, I
found myself on the stage of the theatre, with two
shadowy figures lurking halfway up the stalls behind
an anglepoise lamp. I made my way to centre stage like
a frightened rabbit, saying nothing, until one of them
must obviously have looked up and, seeing that I was
there, began the interview. Many years later I found
out that one of them was the much lamented wonderful theatre director Toby Robertson, but to this day I
never learned the identity of the other shadow sitting
in the stalls.

Taking the initiative and saying 'hello' as you walk into
the room will also encourage people to introduce themselves to you. You wouldn't walk into a room in a social
situation and not greet the people in there, and yet
sometimes when we are nervous or under pressure,
when we feel the spotlight is upon us, our naturally
effective behaviours desert us. We have to consciously
put them back into place. So taking the initiative with
a 'hello' hopefully means that this will be a meeting,
rather than an interview; a conversation rather than an
interrogation.

One of the overriding values that you want to establish
in an effective conversation is that of *trust*. We do this
daily in our lives in conversations with our friends. We
may not consciously know what we are doing, but the
way we conduct the conversations enable people to
trust us and to engage with us. Nerves and tension can
dissipate some of these natural behaviours, and change
the impression we make. One of the most crucial com-
ponents in creating trust is eye contact. Good, effective,
honest eye contact. Think of how you view people who

can't look you in the eye. Make sure you make eye contact with everyone you say 'hello' to and are introduced to. They may or may not offer their hand to shake. Remember, they may be seeing thirty or forty people in the day, and some people in the television and theatre world are known to have limp hands. Let them take the initiative on this, but even if the handshake is not forthcoming, make sure that your 'hello' is paired with a smile and good, direct eye contact.

Although ultimately you are there for this person or team of people to assess your suitability and, in some cases, ability to play the role, you don't want to be placed in the conversation where all you do is answer questions. So don't be afraid to break that conversational mode early on. As you make that 'hello' to the person in the room, or to the director, and you no doubt get a corresponding greeting, continue on with a: 'How are you?' Encourage conversation.

It's also good for you to be able to speak your own name. It helps to associate it with your face in the minds of the people you're meeting. Sometimes you will have been introduced by a person holding open the door announcing you to the room. There still might be room, however, for you to give a: 'Hello, I'm Paul.' If you've been allowed to walk into the room cold, then there's an easy opportunity to say: 'Hello. I'm Paul Clayton.' (Actually, you should probably use your own name, though any work you do acquire by walking into a room and announcing that you're Paul Clayton, I'll be only too happy to take commission on.)

In the civilised world of the television casting, they will most probably ask you to take a seat. Lack of subsidy in theatre means that sometimes there are no seats, and you may be expected to go straight into an audition speech. Lack of manners means that, in a commercial casting, there are never seats, and you will be expected to stand in the middle of the room in front of the camera, where you will then be asked to do an ident.

This involves standing facing the camera, saying your name and agent straight down the lens. Don't feel you have to act this and remember that a smile is worth a thousand words. Most probably you will then be asked to face left and right so that they can see both your profiles on camera. Do this smartly and efficiently. It's a business process. Don't mess around, and above all, don't try and make it memorable. Once, when asked to ident standing next to another actor in a commercial casting, my fellow auditionee decided to show his profiles by doing some mime. He pretended to be looking round a corner as he turned from side to side with much use of hands. I could see him on the monitor and it looked excruciating. My only regret was that it wasn't the normal windy day that mime artists normally go out on. Then he might have been blown away.

Let's go with the favourable option that you have been asked to take a seat. Don't flop into the seat. Don't lounge back to try and give the impression that you're really cool and at ease and laid back and hip, as the perception might be that you are a bit of a tosser (that's a technical term, I believe). Sit up. Look attentive, and listen. The director will probably give you a load of information that they have already given to lots of people during the day, and certainly, if it's the afternoon and you are the thirty-sixth person they've seen, they may well sound bored.

When you're in the room, listen. One of the greatest communicators of the twentieth century, Bill Clinton, said: 'I never learn anything when I'm talking,' and, of course, he's right. It's no accident that *listen* is an anagram of *silent.*

There will probably be a lot of information coming your way, and you will need to take it all in. Lazier directors, even though they're glancing down at your CV on the table in front of them, may well start with the question: 'What have you been up to recently?' Answering this question in a positive way is key, and we will look at that a little later. But, ideally, first of all we want to try and make this a conversation rather than an interrogation.

Building rapport

There is no doubt that the end result of the interview will depend to a large extent on how well you read the role, or perform your audition piece. Having said that, at the end of a casting session, a director can still have more than one person in his head for the role. Quite often, it can come down to the person with whom they feel they would prefer to work, and in most cases this will be the person with whom they feel they have engaged. Engagement means conversation. It's very easy for an interview to be a succession of questions asked by the director or casting director, and a stream of replies from the actor hoping to be cast. If you can break this pattern, and get the director talking, then you can listen, get more information, and there is more chance that you will have a conversation.

People feel good when they are talking. People feel good when they are talking about something that interests them, and let's make a huge assumption here that the project this director is casting is something that interests him or her.

Most job interviews in the real world have a little moment at the end when the interviewer says 'Any questions?' and the interviewee racks their brain for something that they feel is relevant and will mark them out as different. There is a school of advice that says you should always prepare some relevant questions to ask during your interview. As advice goes, it's not bad. Preparing the questions means you're preparing for the interview, and preparation is a key part of success. But planned questions, relevant or not, tend to sound like planned questions. Real questions that come out of the conversation have an authentic ring, and are more likely to engage the person to whom they are addressed.

So what might these questions look like?

Simon Dunmore, the esteemed theatre director and author, relates an anecdote in one of his books of the actor who asked him during an interview '... and what have you been doing recently?' It's a bold turning of the tables, and perhaps far too bold for many people. Evidently he was so taken aback by the question that he not only answered it, but gave the person the job. The trick here is to stay within your comfort zone: to ask what you feel comfortable with. You might get an opportunity to ask them what excited them about the play. Many directors, when castings are running late, will begin with an apology and tell you that they're having a very busy day. You might decide to respond with '... and a successful one?' It gets them talking, and it breaks the pattern.

I went in to do a theatre interview for the rather wonderful theatre director Sarah Esdaile. A chance comment by her, such as 'I hope you're having a good day,' elicited the comment from me: 'Well, I'm glad to be here, because this has got to be better than ringing the O2 customer service line, hasn't it?' If I'd planned it, I couldn't have picked a better subject. Sarah, whose own pet bugbear is call centres, let forth a fabulous tirade of abuse against people in customer-service departments. I had clearly touched a nerve. We chatted on, for several minutes and with a good few expletives changing hands, until the casting director pointed out that we needed to move on and read the script. I did get the job, and in rehearsals Sarah said that the moment that had proved the real point of engagement had been our conversation about call centres. Sure, she had liked my reading, but it was during our conversational exchange that she felt we had bonded, and when it came to making a decision there had been no debate as to who she wanted.

These questions or comments that you will find to turn the interview into a conversation will come from listening. Something that you should be good at as an actor in the first place. But just exactly what does one listen for?

There is a good chance that, in an audition or interview situation, you will be nervous. You may not have had an interview for work for quite some while, and this can increase the pressure considerably. In situations in which we are under pressure, our natural effective behaviours can desert us. Thus, while you may be a good and natural conversationalist with great listening skills when sat with friends in the pub, as soon as you are put in the spotlight, physical or metaphorical, things can change. The best way to remedy this is to focus on one or two positive actions that can put your best and most effective natural behaviours back into place.

Listening can involve keeping an ear out for specific words. Just as any good actor doesn't only wait for the end of the previous line in a script, but analyses what particular word in that previous line is the inspiration for their line, so in conversation specific words can be the cue that you can use and turn into a question.

Asking questions is a mindset that one should try and get into for the interview, but it's difficult, and probably wrong, for me to list particular questions you should ask. More important is the *type* of question you should ask.

In order to get the other person talking in any conversational situation, the use of open questions is vital. An open question is a question that cannot be answered by a simple 'yes' or 'no'. The point of an open question is that the person answering it will give you more information. In life, we tend to ask a lot of closed questions: 'Can you meet me tomorrow?' 'Would you like a coffee?' 'Did I get the job?' All of these elicit a simple and effective answer in the form of 'yes' or 'no'. Yet if we want to get someone talking, a little more is required. Even the questions 'When is a good time to meet?' 'What would you like to drink?' and 'How did I do in the audition?' will all elicit a longer answer than the first version. So good questions begin with 'how', 'what' and 'why'.

In conversational usage 'how' and 'what' are probably the most effective. 'Why' can seem a little interrogative. 'Why are you directing this?' might not endear you to the director, particularly if the answer is: 'For the money!' 'What is it that has drawn you to this play?' would be better. 'How did you come to be directing this play?' – good open questions.

The opportunity for this conversation may come immediately. If it does, then that's good, and allows you to build rapport with the person you're meeting early on. As the day wears on, however, and the interviewer has seen more and more people, your conversation opportunities are more likely to arise as a result of answering the following question...

'And what have you been doing recently?'

Obviously the very best answer to this question is:

> 'I've just finished a six-month run playing Hamlet in a new production directed by Sir Trevor "Take the Money and" Nunn, and while I was doing this, during the day I filmed a new twenty-four-part series for Sky Atlantic about early dwarf settlers in a fictional fantasy land based on Belgium. Other than that, not much, really.'

Sadly, we are very rarely in a position to give that answer, or its more believable equivalent. It is true, however, that work breeds work. The easiest interviews to take part in are those you get while you are in work. So perhaps this may lead you to look at why that is, and what you can do when not in work to replicate this effect. Ask any actor who is in work what they're up to and the first thing they'll tell you is what job they're doing. A job is something you are proud of as an actor. It validates you and gives you a reason to call yourself an actor. It's no problem to walk into an interview room while you're working, because you already know you are an actor. You have proof of it. You're doing a job.

No matter how many jobs you have done, when you go for an interview and you're not working, self-doubt can begin to creep in. So probably the last thing you want to be asked is what you're up to, or what you've been up to, especially if the acting work was a while ago.

Most people don't give enough thought as to how to answer this question before they enter the interview room. The answer to this question can do one of two things:

1. Reveal to the director that you haven't done anything for quite a while, and that your last job is now a distant memory.

2. Encourage you to animate yourself, and allow the director to see and learn something about you as a person.

You should be choosing something appropriate to the job that you're up for. If you're up for a television drama known for its gritty realism, it might not be best to say that the last thing you have done was an open-air production of *Henry V* in Tunbridge Wells. While a passing mention might be good, it would probably be better to highlight the last television work you did. In general terms, theatre people are quite impressed by your television credits if it's given you some sort of profile, and television people are quite impressed by theatre if it's the Almeida. Seriously, though, there is probably very little chance of television people casting in London having seen something you have just done out of town. You don't have to lie – and indeed you shouldn't, as inevitably you will get found out – but you might want to focus the truth in a particular direction. At the time of writing I've just finished a seven-month stint in *Hollyoaks*, the Channel 4 soap opera. I might not be bringing that up in conversation. Given that I have a nice job coming up, my answer to the question might be: 'I've been doing some television and I'm just about to start filming on *Wolf Hall*.' In this way I'm directing their attention away from something I don't want to talk about, to something I do and that I'm actually quite excited about.

So pick something relevant, something that you enjoyed doing, and something from not too long ago, although remember that it doesn't have to be the most recent credit on your CV.

Don't just state the credit as a fact. 'I've just done three episodes of *Casualty*.' They are not asking this as a factual research exercise, they can get that sort of information from your CV. They want you to show some animation and to see a little of what you're like as a person, so make sure your answer has some positive emotional language in it. 'I've just had a brilliant time playing a man with anaphylactic shock in *Casualty*. Three episodes and it turned out to be one of the most fun jobs I've done.' Here you've given them some information they couldn't have learned from the CV, and you also provided an opportunity for them to add on a follow-up question if they wanted. How you phrase the answer to the 'What have you been up to?' question is as important as what you say.

Of course, all the above assumes that you have been in work. It is true for all of us that the interview in which we find it hardest to be ourselves is the one that comes after a six-month famine on the work front. Back in the 1980s, my longest period of unemployment was nine months. It started with good interviews in which I did well without trying too hard. But doing well only got me down to the last two and didn't get me a job. As the months went by, the interviews became harder and harder. They loomed up out of the workless week. Having sat on the other side of the table now on many occasions as a director, casting both theatre productions that I was about to direct, and corporate videos and live events for clients, I have witnessed actors who have come into the room and the overriding impression is one of desperation. Desperation for the work. It's absolutely understandable, and yet unfortunately it clouds our ability to see the person properly. So if this is the situation you find yourself in, your answer to the question needs to be something that allows you to blossom.

> 'Things have been a little quiet on the acting front,
> but I have been spending a couple of months
> working as a bingo caller in the afternoons and
> you should see some of the people I get to meet.'

In that answer, you have not lied. You have quickly acknowledged the fact that you haven't worked for a while, but you have offered information about what you are doing now, and something that may lead the conversation to develop. That's the sort of answer that is not really going to come to you on the spur of the moment. Planning answers to questions is normally not a good idea, but this is one question to which you need to have thought the answer through in order to gain the maximum benefit. If you give the answer above, no director is going to say: 'Stop telling me about your bingo calling, and rake up an acting credit to talk to me about.' Remember, they have asked the question in the first place to get you animated and talking.

When you have something in your mind that you are passionate about or have enjoyed, that will communicate itself and allow you to engage properly with the person you're talking to. Early in December 2008, I returned from a once-in-a-lifetime holiday with my partner in the Maldives. The next day I had an interview for a Channel 4 drama-documentary series about the Queen. Catherine Willis was casting it. She is an absolutely delightful casting director who always makes you feel incredibly welcome at any interview, but she does like things to move forward quickly so she can keep on schedule. I went in to see the director and sat down in front of him and very soon we hit the question: 'What have you been doing recently?' I didn't need any internal debate to find the answer.

'I've just come back from the Maldives,' I said, a huge smile flashing across my face. The director looked up. 'Now that's somewhere I've always wanted to go,' he said. 'What was it like?' There was no holding me back. For the next two minutes I related the joy of a small tramp steamer cruising around uninhabited isles in the Indian Ocean. Spotting a gap, Catherine managed to say: 'I think we might have been talking about work.' The director looked at me and said: 'I think I probably was when I asked the question, but this is much more fascinating. I think I'll have to look it up on the internet and you have to give me the name of the boat again. Now, let's take a look at this script.'

The reading somehow seemed easier. I'm not sure whether that particular director ever went to the Maldives, but I got the job.

So plan the answer to this question, and this question alone. The answer should allow you to talk about something you're happy to talk about. Something you might possibly be passionate about, and something that is relevant, or at the very least, reveals a little more of you the person. Be proud of whatever you're doing at the moment. Actors do a huge variety of jobs in the periods between their appearances on stage or on television. These jobs can give you experience in many walks of life. Certainly they may provide you with anecdotes that will enhance your autobiography. Don't wait till it's published before you share them.

The escape

You should note that, from the director's side of the desk, it is hard to bring an audition to a close. They may have made a preliminary decision by the end of the reading of the script as to whether they have an interest in you. Sometimes the decision is made even earlier. If they are interested in seeing you again, or casting you, then somehow it can be easier to say: 'We're seeing quite a lot of people, but will be in touch as soon as we can.' Because they know they will.

On many occasions when I have been casting, by the end of the interview I will have made up my mind that that person is of no further interest to me, for whatever reason. It's not a decision one likes to make. In an audition or an interview, you want the next person who enters the room to be right. The casting director wants you to be a good choice so it proves that they've done their job well. The director wants you to be right, so that they have the most suitable person for the role and have to look no further. Remember, just before you open the door, you've got the job. From the moment you step into the room there are a variety of points at which the minds of the people making the decision can be changed.

It's never enjoyable to have to communicate what is essentially bad news. Mercifully we are not expected to give a 'no' or 'yes' there and then. But if in your heart you know that you don't intend to see that particular actor again, then finishing the interview can sometimes be difficult. I tend to talk too much, overcompensating for my decision.

So, as an actor, it's important for you to sense when the interview is finishing and to help make that conclusion as clean and effective as possible.

Just before the end of the interview might be the moment when the director has asked you: 'Do you have any questions?' I think there's an unwritten rule here that you should have no more than one question. This might be something you have thought about before you came in. If it is, make sure it's relevant. It hopefully will be a question that has come to you during the interview – checking on dates, starting date, opening date, etc. It's probably best not to raise the question of money, as, whatever it is, it will always probably be less than you were hoping for, and that's a business transaction to be done after you have been offered the job, and by your agent if you have one. This might sound odd, but it is a question I've been asked when interviewing people for theatre jobs. 'What's the company wage?' It suggested to me that their main reason they are doing the job may not be because they want to play the role. Every actor has to run their career as a business, and one part of a business is having the relevant things in your shop window. At an interview, passion for the project is probably one of them, even if this is one of those increasingly prevalent productions where you'll be doing it for nothing.

You may not have a question. This is fine, but you can still turn the moment into something positive.

'Do you have any questions?'

'Actually I don't. You seem to have covered everything, which is fantastic. Thank you.'

Even though you are now thinking about getting out of the room, don't forget to listen. This is the moment when the director or the casting director may well tell you when they will be in touch – which, these days, will most probably only be if you've got the job. No longer do they have the time or the courtesy, it seems, to let people know that they haven't got the job. Three weeks later and along comes the moment when your mind may wander back to the meeting and think: 'I haven't heard about...' Actually you have. You haven't got it. So the remarks made in the last few minutes of the interview can help give you guidance as to when to expect any communication. This can also help you as to how you might follow up the meeting, which we will look at next.

As with most things in life, it's good to say 'thank you'. Don't crawl, and don't over-egg it, but a simple: 'Thank you for your time' or 'Thank you for seeing me' is a polite way of acknowledging that you're pleased to have been there. A handshake may be appropriate, particularly with the person with whom you've been having the conversation. If you feel comfortable, you can initiate this as a way of saying goodbye.

If it is a larger room, then once you've said goodbye, turn and head straight for the exit and go. Don't turn around again at the door to try another goodbye. The director and casting director may well be in discussion by this stage and you could be interrupting. And if you have had the meeting in a larger rehearsal room, make sure you're going out of the right door!

Following up

The very best follow-up for any interview or audition is being able to say 'yes' to the job offer. It's not always an option given to you. More often than not, you will not hear anything more from the people who interviewed you. So was it a waste of time? Not if you follow it up. You may have put in a great deal of work preparing for that interview, and it would be a shame to let it all go to waste.

If the interview was for a casting director you've never met before, then a thank-you card or email is appropriate. In these days of casual electronic communication, a handwritten plain correspondence card, with a brief and simple thank-you message, can be very effective. Casting directors receive hundreds of emails each day, and your carefully composed thank-you email may get the most cursory of glances and then be deleted. It may not even reach the eyes of the casting director, as an overzealous assistant may deem it not important enough to be passed along. A handwritten correspondence card in a handwritten envelope stands a better chance of making it past the gatekeeper and onto the casting director's desk. Don't ask for further work. Don't include phrases such as '... and it would be great if you would consider me for other upcoming roles...', and don't allude to a successful outcome... 'And, of course, it would be great if I get the job and then I can take you for a coffee in Starbucks.' Just say 'thank you'. And these thanks are best after an interview you feel went well. If for some reason the interview was a nightmare, then just leave it.

★★★

Auditioning and interviewing is a skill that is completely different from acting, and as such it requires discipline and technique all of its own. As a young actor you should seize every opportunity to audition that comes your way. As an older actor, don't be afraid to question your suitability for the role. Sometimes casting directors do get people in on a whim, or just to make up their lists. If you feel they are really pushing the boundaries with you and asking you to do something that you feel uncomfortable with or unsuitable for, then ask them, or get your agent to ask them before you go for the interview.

Remember:

- An interview is about letting them see what sort of person you are. It can be the deciding factor when they make their decision on casting.

- Auditions/interviews are an entirely different skill from acting.

- Make the interview element of your meeting a conversation if you can.

- Think about how you will answer that question: 'What have you been doing recently?' in a way that shows you in a good light and is relevant. A good answer might not be about acting work.

- 'Fail to prepare. Prepare to fail.' As good a piece of advice for auditions and interviews as for the job itself.

- Engage them with your conversation. Entertain them with your piece. Bring a performance in with your reading.

Work Task

For your next interview, prepare one of the strategies that we have just looked at.

Positive greetings – can start you off on the right foot and help you through the meeting.

Open questions – can help you turn the interview into a conversation.

Prepare an answer to the 'What have you been up to?' question – it should allow you a chance to show your attitude to things, not just repeat the facts on your CV.

Escape – by being aware of when the meeting is over. Make the other person feel good.

Don't try and do them all. If you do, you will be so focused on that, you may forget to read the script or be yourself.

Take one technique that you feel will work for you and do it in the next interview. If it feels comfortable and good, then great. At the next interview, add one more technique and build up your armoury, one thing at a time.

11. Choosing your speeches

It's easy when preparing for an audition to forget the one quality that undoubtedly will win over the people you're auditioning for: entertain them.

So often people pick an audition speech because they think that the material will 'show off' their acting. But, of course, we never really notice genuinely great acting. When we are in the presence of it in the theatre, we aren't thinking: 'That's great acting.' We are just totally caught up in the story. At the end of the evening we may realise that we've seen a remarkable performance, but rarely at the time.

Audition pieces chosen because the actor feels the speech allows them to run a whole gamut of emotions from A to Z rarely succeed. Tearing out the heart on subjects as unfamiliar to them as rape, child abuse and war rarely come across well in the cold light of an audition room.

The people sitting on the other side of the table may have had to spend the day listening to a catalogue of emotional extremity, and so it's hardly likely that you will endear yourself to them with the use of such material. So often the big emotional speeches from plays are at a point that the audience has had to reach during the previous ninety minutes of performance. It's impossible to access them straight away, and feel their true emotional power in a two-minute splurge.

Material that shows a little humanity, and that raises a smile from the people who are listening, is usually much more effective. It allows them to see you as a believable character, and hopefully a likeable, honest actor – someone they might want to work with.

The people behind the table are willing you to be right for whatever it is they're casting. If they, or their casting director, have done the job correctly, you should be suitable for the role, and what they want to see is who you are.

This can be difficult. It touches on who you are as a person, and it can take years to become comfortable with that. I know that throughout my twenties I went into auditions thinking: 'I'm an actor – what would you like me to be?' As a result I probably came across as nothing in particular, bland and unmemorable. Now I'm perfectly happy to go into an audition room thinking: 'This is me. This is Paul Clayton. This is what I am.'

If I don't get the job it's not because I'm not good. It's because I'm not right. And there's a big difference.

Hugh Jackman was quoted as saying: 'By the time I was twenty-two and started to get into acting, I was shocked at how challenging it was, because the essence of acting is knowing who you are and, at twenty-two, I didn't have any sense of who I was.' That is so true in audition situations. What they want to see is you, and if you haven't decided who you are, then that can be quite difficult. Knowing your own best qualities can be hard. Honesty is good. Say what you actually feel rather than what you feel you should say. There are limits. Telling the director 'It's a terrible script, but I do need the money,' might not hit the spot, but neither will overhyped gushing adoration of material you're not keen on.

Finding material that you think allows your personality to show through can help. That's probably the best criteria for choosing a speech, rather than something that will show off your acting. More than once have I been told by a young actor that they had chosen a piece that they felt was very close to them, only for them to go on and deliver something from a Greek tragedy where they have just slain their mother. I'm never quite sure whether to give them the job or call the CID.

Make use of excellent resources, such as the Mono Box (www.themonobox.co.uk). A truly remarkable and original enterprise, The Mono Box was set up by the actress Joan Iyiola and the movement coach Polly Bennett. They wrote to leading actors and actresses, playwrights and directors, and asked them to send their favourite audition speech with a few notes on why they liked it. They now have a collection of well over 1,000 books which they take to speech surgeries held regularly at the Actors Centre, the Old Vic, and other venues. For a small fee you get a Q&A session with actors and directors about the valuable auditions, and a chance to browse the collection and copy a speech for yourself. The material here is incredibly varied, with lots of original choices. Keep your eye out for something that makes you smile. Or you could even go further – something that makes you laugh. There's comedy in *Hamlet*, remember. It so much easier to see your humanity through a smile.

The Mono Box is worth the investment of a trip to London for one of their sessions, but reading scripts is what it's all about. Samuel French have a brilliant bookshop well worth taking an afternoon to browse in. If London is out of the question or too time consuming, then Nick Hern Books do have the most amazing collection of scripts, from classics to new plays hot off the press, on their website. And if you're lucky enough to live near a still-functioning library, then use it. They can order playtexts for you from other branches if they don't have them in stock.

Finding the right material can take time, sometimes a great deal of time, but it is always worth it. You are the best you there is. Just make sure that your material shows that.

Work Task

Make a list of all the audition speeches you may have used in the past and that you currently use. Write down three qualities that each speech shows of you the actor, and you the person. Look at the list. Where are the gaps? What qualities do you have that these speeches don't illuminate?

Now find at least one new audition speech that allows some of these missing qualities to show through.

Find and learn a new audition speech that is also entertaining.

12. Thinking positively

Opportunities for work can dry up. Weeks or even months can go by without an interview or an audition. When the meeting comes, it can be hard to take your positive qualities into the room rather than your desperation for the job.

The actor Luke Treadaway told me he always goes into an interview believing that he's got the job and that the director has just invited him in to read the part. It's a good mindset to have. Lucinda Syson, the casting director, told me that the difference between many American actors and English actors is that, in America, actors walk into the room as though they've already got the job. It's easy to say, but it's not easy to do. You haven't had a meeting in weeks, and you're trying to make yourself feel on top of your game. Preparation is involved – lots of practical preparation that has been discussed elsewhere in this book – but making sure you have the right mindset for the meeting is incredibly important. Just how do you go about it?

The ability to change how we think is something that has fascinated many people. In the business world, and in many of the corporate training sessions I deliver, there is often a great deal of focus on the techniques of Neurolinguistic programming, or NLP as it's more commonly known. NLP is a technique used by people during times of change when they have to communicate difficult messages, and to help people in their career progression. I haven't trained in NLP and the techniques are something I have only a basic grasp of. I wasn't even sure that these techniques could be of benefit to actors until I saw that an old friend and colleague of mine, the actor Nick Dunning, had developed an NLP course specifically focused on actors and the audition room. Nick is an incredibly successful actor now, with a great CV and almost constant work. We were boys together in repertory theatre in the early 1980s, and he was always someone whose opinion I could trust both professionally and personally. That's why he seemed to be the perfect person for me to turn to and gain a little more understanding about just how NLP techniques can change your approach to auditions.

Auditions can be a living nightmare. They are the doorways from a place of unemployment or temporary jobs into the world of dreams and career fulfilment. It's hardly surprising they are something that actors can get very nervous about, and so much so that many younger actors enter auditions anxious and tense – and, as a result, end up underperforming.

If I had a pound for every time an actor in an audition room has prefaced their reading or their piece with the words 'I'm sorry but I'm very nervous', I'd be heading off down to John Lewis on a spending spree right now. Auditioners and interviewers, if they are any good at their job, know that you are nervous. It's all part of the game. The director you are meeting may well be nervous to. He wants you to be right. There's little point in stating your nerves, but there's a great deal of benefit in doing something about them.

First let's acknowledge that nerves will be there in any situation like this. Nerves are a good thing. They give you edge. They help you find the clever, well-thought-out answer to the difficult question. When nerves impact on your work, however, then it's time to change the way you think. Nerves can tighten the voice. They can give you the shakes, and they can ensure that the reading doesn't go as well as you would hope. One thing is for certain: in the audition room you need to perform to your best potential. Too many times people come out of the room with a feeling of having let themselves down. So just how can you turn this around? How can you do better in the audition room?

I spoke to Nick about how he dealt with this.

'I started to look into the psychology of performance. I figured my mind must have something to do with my poor results. I had this nagging critical voice inside my head that was telling me all kinds of things. I wanted to discover exactly what it is that makes the difference between a good acting audition performance and a poor acting audition performance. And I wanted to see if my results would improve.'

Nick learned that he had what is called a 'poor audition strategy'. Strategies are just a fancy term for the programmes you run inside your mind, your conditioning, based on your education, family circumstances, etc. Your internal programming governs your results – and if you run poor strategies, you get poor results. A little like using a bad recipe when baking: if you mix baking soda, herring and toothpaste, you get a foul-tasting birthday cake. You need to change your ingredients to get a better cake, so you need to change your recipe.

Nick began his investigation with a book called *NLP: The New Technology of Achievement* by Steve Andreas and Charles Faulkner, and tried out some of their ideas for himself. Here is an exercise I found interesting.

Imagine your teeth biting deep into a bright crispy juicy lemon right now and you can feel the sharp lemony juices flowing fast around your mouth. The sharp stinging sensations of setting your teeth on edge.

Now those are just words. Except that as you read those words and try to imagine those sensations, your brain is firing off a series of responses to an experience you already know. Lemons are sharp and sour and taste nasty in close-up. Now erase that for a moment and think of something you love doing. See if you can create positive feelings inside you right now. This is a basic acting exercise. Think of something you absolutely love to do and imagine how you feel when you're doing it. Let that feeling flow inside you. Can you locate it? Is it inside your head? Is it inside your heart? Where exactly is that good feeling located inside your mind or body? Think of those feelings flowing through you. What colour would you like them to be?

Now imagine those feelings growing inside and imagine your next audition going really well, with this warm feeling and colour flowing through your mind and body as you perform easily and well. As you picture your next audition, can you step inside that picture and magnify those colourful feelings and allow the sounds to soften and amplify and swell? Find a phrase to describe the experience. Perhaps a phrase like: 'I love doing this!' Next time you have an audition you can recall this exercise. Just say the key phrase out loud to summon up the feelings you created. 'I love doing this!'

Notice what happens. Notice how good you feel.

This all sounds fine in theory, but from a personal point of view, I remained a little sceptical. Does it work? Nick Dunning again:

> 'The first time it worked for me was auditioning for the movie *Alexander*. I was auditioning for Oliver Stone, and incredibly nervous. I felt I had prepared well using the same techniques. I felt a calm burst of energy as I was in the room and soon I was in the Moroccan desert filming with Colin Farrell and Angelina Jolie. I was thrilled. Things were working. I noticed a sense of improvement in my confidence, in my levels of relaxation, and in my focus and commitment. And something happened that I did not expect. I felt happier than I'd been in ages.'

Looking back on it, he can quantify the results he had from taking these exercises and others into his working life. He developed a system to incorporate these new ideas, a seven-step system he now teaches called 'Total Audition Magician'.

I think the great joy about our work is that many techniques can provide a worthwhile stimulus. You're all different. You are the best you there is. The exercise that works for one person will not work for another, but finding the technique that works for you is time well spent and the results will be worthwhile.

Work Task

As a result of his exploration into the world of NLP, Nick created a video training course, which you can try. Go to www.peak-performance-for-actors.com and sign up. Nick would be really happy for you to leave a comment, and would love to hear from you. Tell him you first read about the course in this book.

Try an exercise from Nick's website. Here is one technique I tried, which I found works for me. It's called Peripheral Vision and evidently originates in Ancient China (quite frankly it could originate behind a bus shelter in downtown Rotherham as long as it helps me in the audition room). It's used today by Formula One drivers to relax them while they're driving the car, and by martial-arts exponents to increase their effectiveness.

When we go into an audition, we are a little stressed. That means we work with tunnel vision, just focusing on one spot. So stand in your room at home and focus on one spot on the wall. Put a mark there, or look at one single small object at eye level in front of you some six to ten feet away. Now raise your arms out to the side, and wiggle your fingers. As you stare at the fixed spot ahead of you, just become aware of your fingers in the periphery of your vision. If you need to, bring your hands a little closer. Note how you feel as you see your hands at the edge of your vision. Then go back into tunnel vision. Stare straight ahead at the marker you have given yourself. Repeat the process two or three more times.

As you open out into peripheral vision, you will feel a sense of relaxation, a sense of commanding the space, and an increased awareness of the room around you.

I found that when I walked into an audition room after doing this exercise, I had a wider awareness of what was going on in there and felt more focused. Perhaps this was just because of doing a simple exercise to focus me, and perhaps any exercise would have done. The fact is, it was this exercise that worked for me, and that's why I believe it might be worth giving it a go.

If you try some of Nick's exercises, make a note in your workbook of the ones that work for you.

13. Joining Equity

It seems that Equity, the actors' trade union, provokes a reaction amongst actors a little like marmite. You either love it or not. I'm going to be very honest. I'm not a fan of Equity. My own career started in the 1970s when getting an Equity card was incredibly difficult. At that time, Equity was a closed shop. You couldn't join it unless you had sufficient paid work, and most jobs were reserved for Equity card holders. It was seen as a barrier to most young actors – something that we had to be part of, but something that didn't seem to want us to join. Even if you had trained on an approved course, the trade union that was to look after you made it very hard to become a member.

In my first year at drama school up in Manchester, several of us were asked to be supernumeraries in the London Festival Ballet production of *Sleeping Beauty*. It was an exciting week, particularly for me as I was given the role of the Prince's guard. When the Prince appeared, his guard appeared behind him holding a spear. As one of the dancers playing the Prince that week was Rudolf Nureyev, the whole week was a great experience. At the end of it, I thought there was no harm in filling out an Equity application form and sending off my contract. Three months later I had heard nothing, so I dropped a line to the Equity office in Manchester. They called and asked what the work was, and a week later, a red plastic wallet and paper receipt dropped through my letterbox. My provisional Equity card.

Another young actor in my year then also applied. Sadly Equity didn't lose his application and responded within three weeks telling him that the work did not qualify him for Equity membership. So, all these years, I suppose I have really been an illegal member. They have had lots of money out of me, and increasingly the cost of subscription is a thorn in my side. I ceased to be a member for six years in my thirties while I was primarily working as a theatre director, but I did rejoin. So why?

The aim of this book is to provide you, the Working Actor, with as many positive suggestions to enhance your career and your work opportunities as possible, so the question I have to ask myself is: 'Is Equity one of them?' My opinion, and it's an entirely personal opinion, is that Equity has to prove its benefits to me. It is just one of many possible tools available to you, the actor, and like most of them it costs money. Is it a worthwhile investement? Recently Equity sent me an email reminding me that my membership was due for renewal. The email listed the political campaigns they were involved in and the support they were giving to trade union matters. Now under the present subscription structure, I am expected to pay a great deal of money for my Equity membership as a result of what I earn. Yet this email asking me to give that money to Equity did not list one single benefit to myself. I replied to it and asked exactly this question: 'Why should I give you money? I want to know what I get out of Equity membership.'

If someone is selling something to me – and that's exactly what Equity are doing with their membership these days – then it's up to them to point out to me the benefits of their product. Given that, as a Working Actor who is successful in financial terms, I am asked to pay a considerable sum of money to Equity, I want to know what I'm getting.

The survey I ran when researching this book gave me 62.9% of respondents who were members of Equity and 37.1% of respondents who were not. The only comments left were from those people who had not had the best of experiences with the union.

> 'I was [a member] for five years and never saw return nor benefit, and I'm now doing just fine without it.'

> 'My acting earnings don't cover the fees.'

> 'I don't see the benefits of it, to be honest.'

> 'I am a member, however I've yet to see any benefit.'

It seems that I'm not the only person to whom Equity is not selling itself well in the twenty-first century.

Couple this with the fact that they are not always as swift in replying as they might be, and I find myself no great fan.

With that in mind, I sat down with Louise Grainger, who is the marketing, events and training manager, to find out just what Equity can do for a working actor to support them. And I have to admit it, I was pleasantly surprised.

The first thing that astounded me when meeting Louise was the sheer range of benefits that Equity offers. I've been an Equity member for thirty-nine years, and there were several things that she introduced me to I had no idea Equity provided. As an actor out of work, you can frequently feel alone. It's easy to see yourself as an out-sider, and if your friends are not working, it can feel hard to have a connection with the world of employ-ment. Equity is one way that you can feel connected. Having an Equity card is a badge of your profession. It's a mark of how seriously you take the whole business.

As an actor who works in lots of fields other than film and television – i.e. corporate and events, training – both outside the profession and within it, I was thrilled to learn that Equity gives me public liability insurance to a considerable level. You may never have thought about having public liability insurance, you may not even know what it is, but given the diverse situations that actors are quite often asked to place themselves in, it is an essential part of your business. Performing in a fringe show, in a small venue, it's not unheard of that, due to being overenergetic during a performance, an actor could injure a member of the audience. (And with some fringe venues these days being slightly smaller than my spice cabinet, I'd say the odds are pretty good.) If the fringe company you're working for is one that is formed by a group of friends, or a new company, they may not have the necessary cover in place should such an unfortunate incident take place, and you could be liable. As an Equity member you are covered, and I quote, 'if solely as a direct result of your activities as an artist, any party brings a claim against you for a) bod-ily injury or property damage, b) personal injury or denial of access; insurers will indemnify you against the sums you have to pay in compensation plus your defence costs.'

This is up to a limit of £10 million. I went online and got a quote for £5 million of public liability insurance, and the premium quoted was £243. Equity are able to negotiate such a good deal because they are buying for a large number of people. Suddenly my subscription starts to look like better value for money.

Louise went on to explain the benefits of Equity's insurance. Full members, she told me:

> 'are all insured automatically, so that is £10 million of public liability. It is accident insurance. If you are injured in an accident at rehearsal, at practice, at a dance class, at work within the entertainment industry, or going to or from. If you are on the No. 9 bus to the National and it crashes and you fall forward and break your wrist, you are still covered because you were going to work.'

One other area that Equity is well noted for is legal support. You may be working without an agent and the world of contracts may be strange and difficult for you to decipher. Equity will look at any member's contract for them. The organisation has worked long and hard to establish standard Equity contracts in most areas of work – fringe, repertory, West End, and film and television. These contracts set minimum rates of pay and standards to avoid exploitation. So, if you have an Equity contract they don't need to look at it as they already know it's fine, but the legal support will come into play on any contract as they can still help you understand what you are signing. What does 'indemnity' mean? What is the reality of doing fourteen shows in five days? What can you say or do or change or mitigate? Equity will take the time to make everything clear for you. It would only take a few hours in a lawyer's office getting this sort of advice before their fee had way exceeded any subscription you're likely to pay to Equity in a year.

All full Equity members have access to the job service. We've looked at this elsewhere, but it's all genuine work that comes straight from the horse's mouth and it's all paid. Equity will carry no unpaid or profit-share work, no 'this would look good on your showreel' work, only paid employment. It might not be cutting-edge television casting, but it's there for you as part of your membership service, and surprisingly few people check it every day.

Equity is a big advice shop. It has an entire training website that you can access as a member. Not training about acting, because Equity has acknowledged that you are an actor and can act – there's an awful lot of training resources on business skills. Marketing yourself. Dealing with the day-to-day impedimenta of running a business. There are also workshops held countrywide throughout the year on different practical skills, like negotiating. If you're thinking of starting your own company, or you are having to deal with employers, how do you negotiate your own rates if you don't have an agent? Equity have two members of staff to look after tax, welfare, and National Insurance advice, help and guidance. They also have a helpline that runs only Mondays and Thursdays, because their staff are quite often individually representing people at tribunals the rest of the week – something they would do for you as a member if you needed it.

There are other benefits and perks that can make an Equity subscription well worthwhile. Discounted car parking with Q Park, for example: you can park in the West End for £6 from six o'clock onwards for an unlimited amount of time with the Equity parking deal. (Check the Equity website for a full list.)

Equity also operates a pension scheme. In these days when the surety of pensions in the future is clouded at the very best, this pension scheme benefits you as your employer will also pay into it. Any job that you do on a standard Equity contract, be it theatre or television, falls under the remit of the Equity pension scheme. Having enrolled, you don't even need to make regular monthly contributions. Each time you sign an Equity contract you fill in your pension details, the contribution is deducted from your salary, balanced by a contribution from your employer. With fees as low as they are on many television jobs these days, it's a hidden and satis-fying way to get just a little bit more out of each job financially. I'm not sure that anybody could actually retire on an Equity pension, but it's certainly a help.

So if you're paying the minimum subscription, which works out at about £10.40 a month, it would seem that you're certainly getting value for money. Insurance, pen-sion rights, career advice, tax advice. You might have to forego three pints or a pair and a half of M&S winter tights, depending on your preference, but in return you will have access to a fantastic range of services.

You can get involved with the political side of Equity, campaigning against arts cuts, pushing for higher min-imum wages, and supporting trade union activities in general, if that's your bag. What I liked finding out is that Equity is primarily a support organisation offering a whole range of services to fully trained professionals. That's what you are. Worth a thought, I think.

Work Task

If you're not a member of Equity, why not take the plunge and try it. You can sign up on the website at www.equity.org.uk and you can pay by direct debit, which you can stop at any time. Once you've joined, you can do the same as those who are already members of Equity, which is log into the Members' Area of the Equity website using your membership number. Work through the perks list (it offers twenty-four different discounts on the day I'm writing this, ranging from restaurants, magazine subscriptions, showreels and massage), and look through the resources available to you. You might be surprised just what you're getting for your subscription.

14. Working with your agent

Let's assume the dream came true. You have got an agent. This may happen directly after your showcase, or it may have taken a little time to achieve. Having spent the first four years of my career without an agent, I was pretty sure that having signed on with someone renowned and influential, the work would come streaming through the door and my life would change. And indeed life did change. I signed with my agent in December 1981 and I didn't work again until September 1982. Not that I wasn't going up for jobs, but just that she had changed the whole type of job I was going up for. The first four years of my career had been spent going from repertory theatre to repertory theatre as a result of the letters I was writing, with a little bit of television slotted in at Granada in Manchester, where I had trained. Now with an agent, I was being put up for plays in the West End, and good-sized roles in television at the BBC. So the opportunities were good, but I just wasn't managing to land any of them.

That's all an agent can do, really: get you in the door. Then it's up to you. It's all too easy as an actor on your own to find other people to blame for a lack of work. Whether the lack of work is coming from you not getting the jobs at interviews, or from the fact that you're simply not getting the interviews, one of the easy solutions is to find someone else at fault. An agent is quite often the first target in the firing line, yet most of us would hate to be without one.

Your relationship with your agent is like any other relationship in your life. It benefits from talking through what both parties want, and how it looks from both sides. Quite often young actors can sign up with an agent and think that all they have to do is sit back and wait for the phone to ring and the interviews to come rolling in. And when they don't... it's the fault of the agent.

When did you last sit down and have a chat with your agent about what you are looking for, what you would like them to do, and what you intend to do? Because you still have to work very hard, even having an agent, otherwise you have handed over entire control of your career to someone else. They may be experienced, and they may have the contacts, but they also have a lot of other clients. They are not there solely for you. They too are running a business. My agent has 190 clients. Given that there are eight hours in her working day, a little simple maths allows me to know that she has about two-and-a-half minutes each day to spend on each client. Multiply that by the four people who work in her office, and it means that I get roughly ten minutes a day. I don't think that is unfair, but it comes as a startling statistic to some people who might think that their agent is labouring on their behalf throughout the working day.

It makes sense that there are things that you can do, and that your agent may expect you to do, that can make the relationship work even better. Amanda

Howard of AHA Talent is my agent, and has been for the last nineteen years. She is quite clear about what she expects of people when she takes them on.

'One of the things that happens, particularly if one has taken on someone young, is that a lot of people don't realise how much they have to continue working for themselves. In a lot of cases, I would say to someone: "You might do better not having an agent. So rather than sign up with someone you don't really like, start by doing it on your own, because you'll make more effort if you do." But we expect someone, when they come to us, to continue operating their own business, as it were. Particularly because, although we do as much as we can for people, there's an awful lot they could still do for themselves.'

The reality is, when you are actively involved in your own career, you will feel much more positive about your progress – even things like keeping your CV and Spotlight entry up to date, keeping in touch with your agent about holidays and any other work you might be doing.

Agents like to see that you are active and take your work seriously. Amanda again:

'We understand that people have got other jobs. That's fine with us so long as we are given the information. There is nothing more annoying for us than if we've got a casting for someone and we find that they're on holiday, they can't get out of work or whatever. As long as we know the information then it's fine. They have to be the judge about how much information they give because we don't want to know they're going to the dentist. There's a lot to do about keeping in touch but we would expect our clients to continue writing letters and keeping in touch with people they've worked with before.'

Given that I work a lot in the corporate market, a field in which my agent doesn't represent me, availability is key. I create a spreadsheet for my agent at the beginning of each month, which shows days where I have bookings that absolutely can't be changed, days when I have bookings that may be changed and my free days. I update this as it changes and make sure that my agent has my availability never less than three weeks in advance. This is something that works for the people in Amanda's office, and means that, in all those years, I think we have only slipped up and had an issue over availability on one occasion.

If you have a television appearance about to be broadcast, then it's a good idea to ask your agent if they are going to be able to do a mailout, or whether that is something that you should take care of. Most agents' websites these days have a news section and that may be where they are intending to post information about your upcoming appearance. You may want to send something a little more personal to casting directors and directors you know, so it's a good idea to let your agent know that you are going to do that. Quite often a personal email from you will probably have more effect than an email from your agent, who, with dozens and dozens of clients, may send out upcoming show information on a regular basis. Your agent can probably advise you about particular casting directors that they think it'd be good to inform. Amanda Howard says:

'I think actors are sometimes nervous that they
don't want to double up with both them and their
agent letting people know about their work. But I
don't think that matters because I think it's much
better for a casting director getting an email from
us and also from an actor than not to get one at all.'

These days you might also think about the format in
which you contact the people you want to see your
show. In an era when everyone is sending emails left,
right and centre, as I have already mentioned, the
power of the handwritten card should not be underes-
timated. A piece of quality stationery with a short
message printed or written on it can get noticed. A
handwritten envelope may well get past the gatekeeper
at the casting director's office. It's worth a try, and
shows that you have made an individual attempt to get
in touch. Keep it professional, even though you're making it personal.

In days of yore when I left drama school, we didn't
even have answering machines, so there was a routine
of calling your agent between 4 p.m. and 5 p.m. each
afternoon to see if anything had come in for the following day. Communication is much simpler and more
immediate nowadays, but just how often should you
call your agent and follow up on things? Malcolm
Browning from Milburn Browning said that when he
first takes people on, he is very happy for them to call
up after a meeting to let him know how it had gone.
Amanda Howard agreed, but pointed out that, as the
relationship develops, it is probably unnecessary to call
each time you have been for a casting:

'I think one of the things that people are very
disappointed to find out is how little feedback they

get after castings. You're quite lucky to hear that
it's a "no", frankly.'

Obviously, if it is something very important, like a
really big role, then the casting director will probably
take the time to speak to your agent if they call them,
but you have to make a judgement call as your agent
hasn't got time to find out about every single meeting
you've been for.

There's also the question of how to behave if you feel
that nothing is happening for you in terms of work.
How often do you call your agent to find out if there's
anything going on? The simple answer is, ask your
agent. It's a professional relationship, just like any other
business relationship, and you need to know what the
parameters are, and then stick to them. Not all agents
feel the need to be your friend. You are a client that
they work for, but it is a professional service.

You might email saying: 'Just feeling out of touch.
Please could you let me know what I'm up for at the
moment?' An email is so much easier for the agent to
deal with than a phone call. It allows them to choose
when they respond. Good agents have a huge database
listing what they have suggested their clients for, and
calling them may not give them the time they need to
look up exactly what you have been suggested for.
There can be a misconception among actors,
particularly if you are with an agent who has a large
client list, that if you don't ring them up, then they
assume you're all right and you may get pushed to the
side. 'Well, so-and-so is all right because they've got
another job teaching.' I think nearly all agents will
tell you that that's not the case. To be successful they
want to have as many of their clients out there

working for them as possible. They too are running a business and they need you to be working in order for them to earn their commission and make their own business successful.

Remember that your agent's office is their workplace. It's not a drop-in centre. If you need to see your agent, then send them an email and make an appointment. Tell them you need fifteen minutes of their time, and then go in and stay for fifteen minutes. You will get fifteen minutes of their sole attention and then they can get back to work, and hopefully you have answers to your questions. I know some young actors who find it incredibly hard to get an appointment to see their agents. I find this rather suspect, unless they're asking for them on a weekly basis. Don't email and say you just want to drop in for a chat if what you actually want to talk about is why you haven't had an interview for seven months. Be open and be honest. You're trusting this person with your career, and you should expect them to be the same with you.

To ensure any relationship works properly, you have to know what the other party wants. I like to cook and my partner is very happy washing up. It makes for happy mealtimes. If you can find out exactly what your agent wants to do, and what they want you to do, then you can both get on with it. In the end, that's probably going to be worth the 12.5% commission.

Work Task

Write a list of what you feel your agent does for you and what you feel your agent should be doing for you. How much do the lists correlate?

Make an appointment for coffee or lunch with your agent. Don't tell them how you want things to work, ask them how they would like the relationship to function. Even if you've been with them a long time, the question 'So what can I do to make our relationship work even better?' is one that they will appreciate. If you have only been with them a little while it's certainly a question you should ask to make sure that you're on the right lines as to how you conduct your association.

Ask them 'What are the things I could do that might turn into work?' Good agents are a fantastic source of information and can often come up with ideas you might never have thought of, and that they don't have time to do. That letter to the National, that postcard to the casting department at the RSC. All things that your agent might think would be a great idea for you to take charge of.

15. Getting great headshots

I absolutely hate having my photograph taken. It's just a fact and it is something I've learned to live with. I can just about cope with it when someone is snapping away on their iPhone, or my partner is trying to catch me unawares when on holiday, and sometimes, just sometimes, the result is pleasing, but in many instances, I note that the photograph does not show the truth as I see it. When I look in the bathroom mirror each morning, I am continually taken by surprise as to just how handsome I am. A sort of Rotherham George Clooney. It's a source of constant mystery to me when I see myself on television, or in a photograph that someone else has taken, that two chins have mysteriously appeared, and some very convincing prosthetics have been applied without my knowledge to make my face the round, moon-like, Benny Hill impersonation it is. I often wonder if people who are naturally striking and handsome spend hours in front of the mirror criticising their looks. It's not a situation I'm familiar with. Everybody looks good in their own way. A good headshot shows that.

So each year, or when I can afford it, the necessity for a new picture arrives. It's an event that I have often approached with hesitation. So much so that on some occasions in my career I have made a photograph last for four years (not something I would advise). These days, just as I am more aware of what I offer as a person, so I am more aware of what I look like in terms of how it comes across on camera. For example, my teeth are set far back in my mouth. Discounting the extra cost that this has added to dentistry over the years, it also means that when I smile, you don't see my teeth. At least the last thing I'm accused of is an unnecessarily cheesy smile, but it does mean that I have a small box of photographs taken during stage appearances where the photographer has caught me unawares while talking, and there's just a large gaping black hole in the lower third of my face.

Your headshot is your calling card. It will say 'hello' to people and get you invitations to the very best meetings way before you actually get to meet the people in the flesh. It needs to be you looking good. That's not you made up to the nines and dripping jewellery (and this applies to girls as well), but you as your most relaxed, genuine self, allowing people to see as much of who you are as possible. Not always easy to achieve perched on a stool in a studio under hot lights and in front of a camera.

I've never been back to the same photographer twice for my headshots. Writing this now and looking back, I think that's probably a conscious decision. Each time, I want reinvention. I want the world to see what someone else sees, and perhaps I want that person to present me to the world in a slightly new way. So how do you choose that particular photographer who's going to do this?

If you're in London, you could go into the Spotlight offices and ask to sit and browse the books. Look through actors in the same category of the book as yourself, actors around the same age. Whose picture do you look at for the longest? Do any pictures catch your eye and you find yourself staying with them for a while? Are you looking at the actor, or are you caught by the photographer's style? I know that in the past I've had at least one headshot which was a great photograph, but more because of how the photograph looked than who was in it. It looked classy, with arty lighting producing high shadow content, and could well have graced an art-gallery wall. Remember, this photograph is to get you work, not the photographer.

If getting into central London is not an option, then look at *Contacts*, where many photographers use shots of previous clients to advertise their work. Or search out photographers' websites and compare images online. Ask friends who enjoyed their session and who feel happy with their headshot.

Having made a list of several photographers you like, now is definitely the time to look at their websites. Remember that these are advertisements for photographers, but you can look at the photographs they display on them and see if they continue to bring out what you liked about the picture you saw in Spotlight. Most people these days encourage you to book a session online, but I would advise you to give the photographer a call and try to speak to them personally. Ask them how long the sessions last. Ask them what they feel you should bring to wear. Their answers may be valuable, but the way they answer the question will be even more so. Which photographer did you enjoy chatting to the most? Perhaps some didn't even return your call or asked an assistant to ring. Just the same way as you might relate to a director at a casting, so you can begin to work out which photographer you might relate to for your headshot.

You should know in advance (or find out if you don't!) the deadline for getting your headshot into Spotlight. When Spotlight existed only as a book, there was an absolute cut-off that actors had to meet, and as a result, headshot photographers the length and breadth of the land would be fully booked in the two or three weeks before. So plan properly. Book the session for at least three weeks *before* you need the photographs. Then treat the session itself as you would an important casting or interview. Don't go out the night before. Don't think you can get your photographs done when you've got a hangover. You are spending good money here. With any top-notch photographer you will be spending several hundred pounds. This is a valid investment in your career, but treat it wisely. It's your headshot that will get you into the room on so many occasions. Just because of the type of person I am, I prefer my sessions to take place late morning. (It is my preferred time for auditions as well if I ever get the choice, so there's the chance to do something afterwards that makes me feel good. I think it's called lunch.)

You will be asked to take along several changes of clothes. Don't leave this until the day when you find that the preferred outfit is lying crumpled and creased at the bottom of the laundry bin. Most photographers agree that plain-coloured clothes are probably best. Stripes and flowery patterns are probably best left for upholstery, and can draw attention from your face or your eyes. Many photographers say they prefer to work with a dark-blue shirt as opposed to a black one, or a cream colour rather than white, as they're less stark and easier to light.

Remember, the photograph is about your face, and nothing should detract from that. If you're busy creating a look (old leather jacket with collar turned up, chunky rugby shirt, suit-and-tie executive – sadly all of those come from my own experience) you'll have to take that look into the casting room every time. If the photograph is about the face, chances are you'll have that face with you on every casting you go to. What you do with your face during the shoot is what's important.

One of the more entertaining games when sitting in a theatre green room used to be to find a copy of Spotlight, and flick through the pages for examples of people gurning for the camera to demonstrate their ability. No less a crime is to sit in front of the camera and do nothing. A good photographer will talk to you about what your thoughts should be as you look into the lens. It's purely a matter of personal taste, but I get bored very easily by the type of pictures that lots of graduates have as their first Spotlight photograph. Looking straight down the lens, possibly no hint of a smile, and just trying to portray 'I'm an actor.' It's understandable. Many graduates at this point are trying to convince themselves of that fact as well as the people who are looking at the photograph. As I've said on other occasions in this book in regard to other topics, people buy people. When looking at a headshot, most people want to feel that the photograph is looking back and engaging with them. It doesn't need to be a big, wide, cheesy grin (though a hint of a smile is always so much more welcome than a sulky pout), but what one is looking for is a hint of your own charisma.

Some drama schools launch their graduates into the world, having spent three years teaching them self-belief and encouraging them to make individual decisions, by sending them all to the same headshot photographer for their showcase brochure. Thirty-four people (and that's assuming you went to one of the drama schools with a small final year!) all photographed by the same person in basically the same lighting conditions on the same day. Look at the websites of drama schools, click on their graduates gallery, and see what style they use.

In the days when photographers used film, they would shoot two rolls of photographs, process the contact sheets, and send them out to you. Your choice would be made from seventy-two photographs. Given that you would have blinked or gone slightly cross-eyed on at least five, your choice was limited, and easier to make. These days, in the digital heaven that is the twenty-first century, the photographer can email you through up to two hundred shots. When choosing your photographer, don't be impressed by the number of shots they say they will send you. More is not necessarily better. Several photographers I have used have sat down with me at the end of the session and taken me through the shots on their computer, deleting some as we go. There'll be at least twenty-five per cent of shots that you probably can say goodbye to very quickly. Many shots will replicate others, but with just a tiny change of eye contact, or a small alteration in the placement of one of the chins. You need to reduce the number of shots from which you are going to make your final selection down to about ten or twelve. Whatever you do, don't send your agent the digital contact sheet containing all two hundred photographs. Agents, no matter how caring and concerned about your career they are, just do not have time to look through that many photographs.

I firmly believe that I am not the right person to choose a photograph that sells me. Ultimately, my agent is that person and I always leave the final choice of headshot to them. I would tend to say don't ask friends, but ask other actors, or friends who are actors if you have acquired any. If you're working on something at the moment, ask an actor or a director if they have a minute to make a quick choice from your shortlist. Having some idea now as to which of the pictures are getting the best reaction, send the contacts through to your agent. You should compress the file. Ten high-res images can often produce an email that might get blocked by your agent's server, or take them a long time to download on a mobile device.

Mercifully, these days, most of the casting services allow you to exhibit more than one photograph. It is possible to have several images on Spotlight, both colour and black-and-white, so the choice does become easier. My agent is the person who sells me, so I let them choose what they want to put in the shop window. I always pick one picture that I like. It's probably one that makes me look younger and shows my George Clooney side. I don't send it out for jobs, but if people need a picture of me for publicity, to display outside the theatre, or to accompany an article or on the back of a book (!), then that's the one I let them use. There is absolutely nothing wrong with a little bit of vanity if it's in the right place. That one personal picture is usually colour. There is an increasing tendency these days for colour pictures to be asked for, but the classic professional headshot is still black-and-white. While it's perfectly possible to get colour pictures sent to you from the photographer and to turn them into black-and-white prints using a photographic editing programme on your computer, you might find it easier to just check with the photographer when booking the session that you will get high-res images in both colour and black-and-white.

After all this work, the objective is to have chosen a headshot that will get you jobs. A headshot that will get you meetings. Make sure that when you walk into the room you live up to the photograph. The reason they want to see you is that they liked the photograph, so it's probably a good bet on a first meeting to make sure that's what comes into the room. Casting a play in the mid-nineties, I had a leading actor who sat in on several days of auditions. It was a little bit of a novelty for him, and it wasn't long before he started taking great delight in holding up the headshot of the next applicant so that he had the photograph in his eyeline as they walked in the door. On more occasions than not, he harrumphed in disappointment as the real person entered the room. On some occasions he was reduced to a comedy double-take, and in one moment of great truth, but toe-curling embarrassment for the rest of us, he held out the photograph of one actor and asked him: 'Could your brother not come?' Rude, but right.

You are the best you there is. Your photograph should show this.

Work Task

Work out when you need to have your headshots taken or renewed and put a date in the diary now. Quite often, photographers will do a deal at less busy times of the year. Some photographers even let two actors share a session, so the two hundred or so images that you get can be shared between yourself and a friend.

If you're a member of an organisation such as the Actors Centre or The Actors' Guild, they will probably have photographers offering a discount on their perks schemes.

Start looking at lots of photographs of other actors and find shots that you like. Drop photographers a line and ask when would be a good time for a chat.

If you have had several headshots already during your career, look back at them and ask if any particular one was more successful than the others in getting you work. Ask yourself why? Did that look suit your age? Was it a particular style?

See which photographers do trial shoots at reduced prices. The more time you invest in preparing, the more likely your headshots will deliver what you need.

16. Working with casting directors

It's always good to remember that casting directors can't get you jobs. Only you can do that. What casting directors *can* get you are interviews and meetings. They are the people who are in control of who gets in the audition room, which is why actors perceive them as people with all the power. But actually, *you* have all the power. It's your work that will get you the job. The casting director is the gatekeeper, the person who makes sure that the director gets to see people who are suitable for the role. If you're not getting seen by a particular casting director, then it's not unusual to think of them as narrow-minded, and shortsighted. If you are being given interviews by a particular casting director, then it's easy to see them as a professional facilitator who is providing space for you to do your job.

Actors are probably the worst people for casting themselves. It's hard to be objective when you're desperate. It's hard to say 'I'm not right for that,' when you haven't worked for four months. As one casting director told me:

> 'I've had breakdowns published in industry publications and I have physically not been able to manage the response. Ninety-five per cent of those are from actors, not agents. They are

inappropriately submitting themselves because they are the wrong age or type. They're not looking at the brief. You ask for someone with a disability and they say: "Well, I broke my ankle once so I know what it's like to walk with a limp."'

So just what do the casting directors want? What are the things that you can do that will enamour you to them and get you into their minds? After all, if a casting director has a choice between an unknown quantity and an actor he or she knows does good interviews and regularly gets jobs, they are more likely to call that person in. A casting director has a job to do, and they have to do it well.

Getting advice from casting directors is incredibly valuable. Understanding how they work can help you understand what they need. I talked to two prolific casting directors to try and get a heads-up on just what they are looking for when they meet you. Hannah Miller is currently the head of casting at the Royal Shakespeare Company, having previously worked as a casting assistant at the National Theatre, deputy casting director at the RSC and casting director for Birmingham Rep. She's also cast productions for Northampton Theatres, Hampstead Theatre and the Young Vic, and she regularly works in drama schools and with other industry organisations advising actors on professional development. Catherine Willis is a freelance casting director whose career started out in theatre and then went on to include six years' in-house casting at the BBC drama department, where she worked on such programmes as *Casualty* and *Waking the Dead*. She began as an independent casting director in 2006 and specialises in new series, both drama and comedy, and has a strong line in critically acclaimed drama documentaries. Recent credits include *Truckers* (BBC One), *Dates* and *Fresh Meat* (Channel 4), and *Mount Pleasant* (Sky).

What I like about Hannah and Catherine is that they are unequivocal about the fact that they are both there to help the actor. They need to do their job to the best of their ability, which means putting the most suitable actors forward, and making sure that the director has an interesting mix of people to see for each part – whether it's three lines in a sitcom for Channel 4 or a number of parts in the season at Stratford.

Casting is an area in which increasingly everybody has an opinion. Directors, producers, the network – it's even been known for the wardrobe designer to email suggestions for particular parts to the casting director. That's why the casting director needs to be sure they're putting the right actors in front of the director for the right parts. It's their opinion that is valued, and that opinion is gained by acquainting themselves with the work of lots of different actors, by watching their performances, by looking at showreels, by talking to agents they respect, and by using their own highly tuned instincts.

It's very easy to think of casting directors as the enemy – the doctor's receptionist of the acting world. You may be relatively inexperienced and you may be agentless, but as Hannah Miller says: 'The most important thing to remember, if you do come out of drama school unrepresented, is that agents don't give you auditions and certainly don't give you jobs.'

It's the casting director who will give you this opportunity, so it's much more important for you to keep in touch with casting directors who came to see your showcase than it is the agents, because they are the people who will invite you in for the audition and hopefully will have seen your work.

So how should you keep in touch? Hannah prefers email:

'We are moving more and more to just email. It helps us cope with the numbers. We do have a separate email account which all members of the casting team here at the RSC can access and that's the one we advertise in *Contacts*. It's really important to remember it's a professional contact, so write the email as you would a letter, but similarly be brief and to the point. I was given some good advice a long time ago that any covering letter is a bit of a trailer for the CV. It should make me want to turn over and look at the photo and the CV that comes with it. So an email should make me want to scroll down or open the attachment.'

Catherine is in agreement:

'I get emails every day and I get hard copy every day, which is fine. It's great that people are so proactive. What does worry me about some actors is the amount of money they waste by doing that.'

By 'waste', she is referring to the people who go through *Contacts* and send their CV and photograph – 'Dear Sir/Madam' – to at least fifty different casting directors. These people are not 'Dear Sir or Madam'. Why would anyone be interested in the letter that opened with that? Know or have an idea of what you're good at, what you want to do or what you think you can do. Write to ten casting directors, but tell them why they should be interested in you. 'I want to do comedy,' or 'I really like this drama that you do and I think that's the kind of thing I'd be good for.' Give them something to hook onto, otherwise you'll just come across as another one of the 40,000 people trying to get a job at the moment. It's a case of being as specific as you can when you're writing any letter or application because the 'Dear Sir' approach just doesn't work. As Catherine says:

> 'If I open an email or letter which says "Dear Catherine Willis, I really feel the kind of work you do on projects such as this and this is what suits me," then I'm thinking: "Okay. Well, I've got a second series of both of those coming up. Let me have a look and see."'

It is also very important to make sure that your request is as specific as possible. Every single actor can say: 'Give me a job!' or 'Can I have a general meeting?' But no casting director can meet everybody. It really is about trying to pick a moment where you've got a bit more to say than that, whether it's 'Come and see me in the show,' sending reviews of the show, 'I'll be on television,' or 'I know you're casting this, this, and this. Please see me for this, this, and this.' Pitch for a role that you know is actually open and then you're more likely to get a response.

Both Hannah and Catherine are very keen on keeping it all professional. Don't do the gimmicky thing. You might think it's great to send me a teabag and say: 'Let's have a cup of tea' – but only you will really know where that teabag has been. Remember, it's a job interview.

Getting 'into the room' throws up its own set of problems, and casting directors do like people to deal with it in their own particular way. As an actor you need to be prepared for anything, and if you are prepared, then you can probably cope with anything that is thrown at you in the meeting – whether it be a new script interpretation, or walking in to see many more people than you anticipated.

Preparation means different things to different people, which is why it is difficult to lay down any golden rules. Do everything within your power to make sure that when you come out of the room you have no regrets. Don't regret arriving five minutes late – leave earlier. Don't regret having not prepared the script enough – find the time. Some things will be out of your control: you can't do anything about the train that breaks down, but you could have left the house earlier to build in some contingency time. Look at the weather – if it's likely to rain, take an umbrella so you don't arrive looking like a drowned rat. All things that are nothing to do with the audition itself, but just ensuring that you'll feel better, look better, and probably do better, in the interview itself. Don't go out the night before, or don't agree to an early appointment if you have got something on the night before and you don't really want to be on an early train. Ask about the time slots available. The casting director may say that the last appointment they have is twelve o'clock and you know that you will have to pay through the nose for a rail ticket. You just have to make the call. At least if you've asked you know you've given yourself the best opportunity to get on a train at a reasonable cost and at a reasonable time. Just make sure that you're not walking away from the job audition feeling: 'Oh I wish I had...' As Hannah says:

'I think the best auditions are where someone is absolutely confident that they know how to deliver on it. They know that this is their part and they take on complete ownership. They've put the

153

work in and absolutely want to prove to you that this is for them.'

When you walk into the room to meet a casting director, you are a professional coming in for a job interview. Even if you give an amazing read of the script, if you don't emanate the sense that you're a professional, reliable, responsible actor, it can sow a seed of doubt in the director's mind. They might start to wonder if they want to work with you. Casting directors increasingly send out requests for auditions at the last minute. I'm pretty sure that they knew they had the casting before that moment, and you might regard sending scripts to actors the night before as unfair, and a little sadistic. Sadly, if this is what happens, then you have to make it work in your favour. Because if you don't, someone else will. If they send you the whole script, then read it.

Learn the lines if you can, but a casting isn't a memory test. You should be familiar enough with the dialogue that you can lift it up so that the camera can see what you're doing. What they want to see is what you're bringing emotionally. You don't have to get it absolutely right in the audition and, in fact, if the people who are seeing you know what they're doing, they wouldn't expect it. Directors who need you to absolutely nail the moment will give you that chance and ask you to do it again. The important thing is that people want you to come into the room with an opinion. It's hard because you want to come in being whatever they're looking for, but on many occasions, directors don't always know. The fact that you made an intellectual decision about the character can be very inspiring. In casting for the theatre, Hannah Miller is also keen to point out the fine line about actors having to be off-script. 'We're not doing a memory test. Many times people have thought that they knew it, and the line goes, and it all just becomes about remembering it.' Have the script in your hand if it's going to give you more confidence, but just don't let it block people seeing what you're doing.

Both casting directors told me that they are quite often amazed how actors in interview aren't really listening to them, and are reinterpreting the questions asked through a film of terror, concern, anxiety, and assumption. It's very easy to become desperate to say what you wanted to say, rather than actually giving the answer to the question that was asked. The casting director and the director are not trying to trick you. They want conversation in order to find out a little more about you as a person, because at the end of the day any director is trying to decide who will fit best with the team they are assembling on this particular job.

One interesting practical point that Catherine pointed out is that ninety per cent of the castings you do probably involve sitting on a chair. The chair will already be in place when you enter the room and that's where you'll sit by default. There might be a very practical reason (such as blue screen, or a white background) as to why the casting director wants you to sit in the chair, but if you do feel you might do better standing up, then ask. Catherine again:

'I think sometimes if they need that extra energy in a scene, then it will be on its feet, so then yes, do ask the question. Make sure you know why you're standing up though. Nothing worse than somebody who says: "May I stand up?" And then they stand up and look down and don't know what to do with their hands, and make everybody in the room think: "Why didn't you stay in the chair?"'

Casting directors have to be rigorous. They have to demand the highest professional standards. Actors who don't meet these standards won't get invited back for repeat interviews. They want you to do well in the room as it reflects well on their abilities. To that extent, they are on your side. They want to learn about new actors, but they don't necessarily want to spend every evening of their lives in a theatre above a pub finding them. They want to be able to put the best possible people in front of the directors they are working with. And when they get those actors there, they want to be able to rely on them. To trust them. To know that they will deliver.

Work Task

Make a casting checklist. Do it before the next casting comes in so it is there for you to refer to.

Just what will it take for you to feel well prepared?

Make a list of the casting directors you have met, and what you have met them for.

Make a list of the casting directors you would like to meet, and why. Using online resources such as the Casting Directors' Guild website, Spotlight, and search engines, check whether any of these casting directors work together. Quite often two casting directors may work on one particular series. If this is the case and you have already met or worked for one of them, it could give you the necessary 'in' that you need to drop a line to the other.

17. Being a geek (with apps for actors)

My name is Paul Clayton and I am a geek. That may come as a revelation to some people, and it sounds like a declaration that one might have to make at a self-help group, but ever since I was persuaded to buy my first laptop with a massive 3GB hard drive in 1999, I have been hooked on technology and all things computer-related. I turn on my desktop first thing in the morning, and I turn it off last thing at night. It is a window on the world, a source of endless possibilities. The internet may be for porn, as Trekkie Monster and the cast of *Avenue Q* would have us believe, but it's also for work and opportunity, and as such enables the Working Actor to have more control over information, opportunities, and their career. I have a laptop, two iPads and a smartphone, and they all play their role in my working life. They are not essential by any means, but they make things easier and, in some cases, have become invaluable. Whether it's online banking or social media, apps play a big part in our lives already. They can also provide great shortcuts in your working day, and opportunities for professional development that you can take advantage of on your own.

Working on any film or television set these days you will see actors using their smartphones and tablets for a variety of activities. Keeping in touch with the real world, catching up on an ebook, passing the time away between shots with a quick game of Candy Crush Saga. (It should be pointed out that this game is probably as addictive as a class-A drug, and should most definitely be avoided. Even MPs have been known to fall victim to it.) The days of a group of actors sitting round with pencil and paper playing 'Boxes' or other such home-made games seem long gone. Of course, all this is dependent on phone service. I recently just completed filming on a large historical epic where all the locations seemed to have been picked with two criteria in mind. First that they were a castle, and secondly, that they were without any phone service whatsoever. Incredibly frustrating for an awful lot of people who wanted to spend their lunch hour checking emails, etc. – and for Darren the driver, whose car had built in WiFi, and who suddenly became immensely popular.

Here are some of the apps available at the time of writing that you might use in your working life to make things just that little bit easier. And a few of my own independent thoughts on each.

The Stage

The Stage has an app you can download for free. This is different from the electronic edition of the newspaper, which you need to subscribe to. The app lists jobs, but like the newspaper itself now, you probably won't find any 'real' acting jobs listed here. Unless you're looking for something in a holiday camp or on a cruise ship, this won't be your first point of call for casting information. You'd be much better off subscribing to the newspaper and having the full version of that on your tablet. It's a great read.

LineLearner

When you say to people that you're an actor, the second question they will ask you (after: 'What have you been in?') is most probably: 'How do you learn your lines?' As a young actor I never had any problem learning lines. An afternoon rehearsal, a quick look through the script before bedtime, and the lines were in there, word perfect, for the next morning. Now it takes me longer. Much longer. I have to work at it, and considering that the art of acting, according to Noël Coward, is to learn the lines and not to bump into the furniture, turning up knowing the words is at least fifty per cent of the job. Personally I find it very helpful for castings, where I need to be familiar with the lines and very often scripts are sent out at the last minute. The actor who gets the job will be an actor who was very comfortable with the lines when he did the reading.

The app LineLearner is a brilliant way to learn lines for a play, or an audition. You speak each line into your smartphone and, as you do so, you press a button to distinguish whether it's your line or another character's line. Once you have read a short scene, you can start practising. In playback mode you will hear the other characters' lines to cue you in, and then a pause before your line to allow you to speak it out loud. The recording then plays the correct line. You can press a button to receive a prompt. Or you can just play the whole of the dialogue through and listen to it in order to get to know your lines at first. The app provides space for each scene to be separately recorded. It's easy to edit a scene, or to re-record a single line, or the whole scene if you wish to. You can have as many different scripts in the app as you like.

Available for both iPhone and Android, at around £2.50 I think it's an absolute steal, but there is a free version available which will allow you to record up to ten lines and test it out to see whether it is for you – always a good thing. I can record the scene easily, on the move if necessary, and then I spend a good twenty or thirty minutes just listening to the lines going round and round in my head. Then I move on to playback mode with a pause before my lines, and find that I suddenly know more than I thought. When I completed a seven-month stint on a soap opera, it was this app that proved invaluable with the huge amount of last-minute line-learning required. *The Stage* has also just released Lines2memory, which is essentially the same as LineLearner.

Rehearsal 2

Right up there with LineLearner in my own personal digital armoury is Rehearsal, or Rehearsal 2 as it is now labelled. Developed by the imperiously named American actor David H. Lawrence XVII, it's a fantastic way of importing whole scripts, audition speeches, or daily film sides onto your iPad and iPhone. (David says there is no real intention to develop an Android version of this, so at the moment, it's an iOS app only.) Once you purchase the app, one of the pricier ones I am recommending at £13.99, you create an account. This gives you an email address that you can send scripts to as PDF or Word documents, which open in your app. By doing this you can have the scripts on all devices, but you can also just open a script directly from an email into the app on the device you're using. I mainly use this app on my iPad, and find it exceptionally useful.

The app allows you to annotate digitally any imported scripts. You have digital highlighter pens, and a pencil that you can use to make notes and mark up your scripts as you want them. You can record your lines and play them back, and the script will roll past you like an autocue. You can also set the script to automatically repeat one scene. The audio option isn't quite as impressive as LineLearner, as you have to read your lines silently, and those of the other characters at full volume. What is impressive is that at the touch of a button, the app will blank out all your lines on the script, just leaving those of the other characters showing. So instead of having to run down your physical script with your hand, or an unwanted first-night card covering line after line, here you have an instant cover-up. The good thing is that you can also increase the font size by making the document larger, exceptionally useful for those of us who have reached a certain age, and also very helpful to you if you are using the app as a surreptitious prompt.

The app also allows you to add other media and documents to your script, which can be very handy during the rehearsal process. It's incredibly useful if you have several scripts on the go at the same time, as it means your work bag isn't filled up with dog-eared paper scripts. As I was writing this chapter, my agent phoned with an audition for two o'clock the following day. I opened the script in Rehearsal 2 from the email she sent, and, actually, using a combination of this app and LineLearner, I was word perfect by that evening on quite a complicated and wordy scene.

These days most castings expect you to have printed off the sides at home and turn up with your own copy. I do remember turning up for the first time with the sides on my iPad, and thinking it might look a little pretentious or frivolous, and so on going into the room I picked up a paper copy. The director did ask me: 'Why the iPad?' and I told him that I had my script on it, but suddenly lost my nerve to use it at the last moment. He took one look at the app, and thought it was brilliant. 'I'm going to download that,' he said, and as a result, I take scripts on my iPad into auditions all the time now.

David H. Lawrence XVII has provided a lot of video support for the app, and also provides great technical support by email. No free trial on Rehearsal 2, I'm afraid, but you can look up how it works by searching for Rehearsal 2 online. There are a huge number of testimonials on the website, and it does give you screenshots so that you can get an idea of how the app works in action. Best to download it from the App Store, though, and one download on your iPad also means you can use it on your iPhone as well.

Shakespeare/Shakespeare Pro

You may have a *Complete Works of Shakespeare* on your shelves somewhere, or a couple of Arden or New Penguin Shakespeare editions for any plays that you have studied or appeared in. Shakespeare is a free app that gives you his *Complete Works* on your digital device in a searchable format. It allows you to change the font size, the font colour, and find text by character, or by quotes. Great for any readings or workshops, and fantastic for when that RSC audition comes along for which you need a new and interesting piece. As well as the thirty-seven plays we commonly associate with Will, the app also contains plays which he possibly wrote or collaborated on, such as *Double Falsehood*,

Edward III, Sir Thomas More, The Two Noble Kinsmen, as well as all the sonnets and longer poems.

There is a facility with which you can tap on any word to see its definition, although one should bear in mind that this app is of American origin and that may be reflected in some of the definitions. It is certainly a huge resource that is available to you absolutely free. For £6.99 you can upgrade to the Shakespeare Pro, which gives you a lot of added functionality, such as the ability to highlight text; to make notes on the text and share them; to add bookmarks; to auto-scroll the text, which can be very useful for learning or preparing a speech; and includes extras such as twenty short versions of Shakespeare's plays aimed at the younger audience.

Oxford Dictionary

There are lots of free dictionaries available as apps for you to download, and of course your word-processing programme will have its own spell check and thesaurus, but quite frankly the *Oxford English Dictionary* is the best. Whether you're using it to help you understand a difficult text, or using it to find that perfect word to finesse an (individually) written letter to a casting director, it's something every actor should have access to. For so many of us, words are our trade, our tools. Knowing more of them, and how to use them effectively, can only enhance the power we have over language.

The Accent Kit and The Real Accent App

I have been very lucky and managed to build a career by doing posh, Northern, and posh Northern. Accents have been something that have never really figured in my thinking, or been required for my career. I have a passable Scottish accent which surfaced in a children's television series in the late nineties, and more recently made a repeat appearance in a radio horror. My American accent is absolutely dreadful, and I have a Mittel European accent that has been used in corporate training, but is less likely to grace a Bond film. So when I came across a pair of apps, The Accent Kit and The Real Accent App, I was intrigued.

The Accent Kit has been put together by three of the UK's leading accent coaches, and describes itself as an invaluable resource for actors, or anyone wanting to learn an accent. It's free to download and gives you access to a whole library of authentic accent speakers chosen for their authenticity and 'usability'. The app, compiled by Edda Sharpe, Jan Haydn Rowles and Richard Ryder, comes with just one accent pre-installed: the Cornish accent as spoken in Truro. (Whether this is in response to the catastrophe known as the BBC adaptation of *Jamaica Inn*, I'm not sure, but it's certainly not an accent that I've had a need to call upon, although Truro itself is quite pleasant and certainly worthy of a weekend break. If I do ever need to learn it, I will know where to turn.) The idea here is that you buy the accents as you need them. 'Sheffield male aged sixty-six born 1948' seemed authentic enough. The app breaks each accent down into free speech; speaker telling a one- to three-minute story of personal interest; foundations, which look at the setting, zone, and tone of the accent; vowels, the vowel sounds that give you the shape of the accent; and consonant sentences, which contain the six key consonant sounds that can make or break your authenticity. Following this there is a practice text where the native speaker reads a text (combining all the speech sounds of the accent) for you to practise. Always check the online reviews to read about current updates, etc., but this is an app that is certainly worth looking at... or should that be listening to?

The Real Accent App works in a similar way, with various native speakers for each accent. There are different versions of this app for American accents, English accents, and what are referred to as the 'Celtic nations'. One price, one purchase, and you get ten full accents in each app. It has lots of nice features, such as an innovative function that records your voice and compares it to a native speaker's, and a 'Test Your Ear' quiz that helps your listening skills. If you're looking for one of the ten accents featured in that particular app, then this really is worth considering. If you're looking for something a little more specific (i.e. Truro), you may need to look elsewhere. There is no free trial on this app, so you do have to pay the full price to find out if you like it.

Being in Voice

I have to confess: I'm not as brilliant at doing vocal warm-ups as I should be. In the mid- to late 1980s when I played Claudius in *Hamlet* at the Young Vic, we had some morning performances for schools, and my vocal warm-up consisted of two Benson & Hedges. These days I spend my time growling or mumbling my way through various television performances. On my last stint in the theatre, my voice began to wobble seriously after only three public performances, and it took a Sunday of rest and a regime of strengthening exercises to keep it fit for the rest of the run. Had I had a warm-up app, I might have been more conscientious about keeping my voice in peak conditon at all times. Most of the apps I looked at concentrated on singers, and were designed as warm-ups for a musical performance. As such, they do no harm, but if, like me, you can turn cats neurotic at twenty paces with your singing voice, then those are not the sort of exercises you might want to do when anybody is within hearing. The exercises used in Being in Voice are more designed for the speaker. It contains many warm-ups, and a longer, more general vocal warm-up, which actually takes you back through some of the principles that you will have done in training about how the voice works and how breath works. These exercises might be a little basic for you, but it probably does none of us any harm to be reminded. With exercises on articulation and tone, this is a good all-round vocal app. After all, having spent money on it, it may just get you into the habit of warming up and doing vocal exercises every day, which is a productive thing to be doing as part of your day, even when not working.

Actions: The Actors' Thesaurus

My book doesn't address the process of acting, rather it's looking at all the things you need to support you day to day as an actor. However, the Actions app is one that can be incredibly useful in the rehearsal room. You may have used actioning in your training, and, if you have, you will know how much it can help in breaking down text in terms of your acting choices.

Actors need actions. You cannot act moods. You need to be doing something with every line. You need to have an aim to achieve and you need to have selected an action to achieve that aim. Actions are active or transitive verbs. In order to play a line truthfully you need to discover the action that suits that particular situation and their particular line. That's where this app can really help. Your actioning can be limited by your vocabulary unless you have easy access to a thesaurus, and that's not the easiest of books to carry around in a rehearsal room. This app is a fully searchable, easily navigable thesaurus of active verbs that will help you refine your acting choices until you find the action required to make the lines come alive. In the app, the verbs are placed in emotional groupings to help you pinpoint the action you require, and there's a really easy-to-use alphabetical search function. There are full instructions on how to make actioning work for you in the rehearsal room, and, of course, full instructions on how to use the app. I found it very simple to navigate my way around. It's great that it's on my phone as it is easily and discreetly accessible. (Just make sure that the director doesn't think you are texting your agent to get out of the job!) Finding the right verb for the right line can sometimes shine a light into what you're doing in a scene. This app puts an immense word power right in the palm of your hand.

Work Task

Download the LineLearner app and give it a free try with a short scene.

Download the free version of Shakespeare Pro and have a good old look around. Find a Shakespeare speech that you worked on before, and just for the sheer hell of it, highlight it in a different colour and read it out loud. If you're currently not in a job, then find a new speech, speak it, and learn it. Always good to have another speech in your pocket.

Using your dictionary app, set yourself a target to learn a new word, and how you might use it in conversation. Maybe once a day, or once a week, or once a month. Challenge yourself that by the end of that day you have to use the word at some point in conversation or writing. For instance, why not pop into Sainsbury's and say 'What a fabulous gallimaufry of packet soups you have!' You don't necessarily have to use the word out loud or to someone else, but extra points if you do. Now if that's not got you reaching for your dictionary app...

Check out the website at www.theaccentkit.com, download The Accent Kit now, and have a trial run on your Truro accent. By my calculation, there are several more series of *Poldark* to hit our screens.

The apps mentioned in this chapter are just a taster to get you started on making technology part of your working life. There is an incredible amount of support for actors out there now. Websites, such as the Honest Actors Podcast and Blog, Twitter feeds, and a huge variety of printed material, all set out to support the actor and are well worth perusing. Set yourself a couple of hours to come up with a list of content that you would like to buy and add it to your next birthday or Christmas list. After all, anything that makes your working life a little easier, and a little more focused, has to be a good thing. It frees up time for you to do other activities, and the more you do, the more productive you will become.

18. Working whilst resting

There are very few actors who can hold up their hands and say they haven't had to do 'a bit on the side'. I'm pretty sure that Dame Judi Dench hasn't had to take to the tills at Aldi, but there are distinct rumours that Benedict Cumberbatch did a mean demonstration of a mascara wand on the Revlon counter at the Windsor and Eton branch of Boots. Perhaps we'll never hear more. In my first stint out of work I lasted one morning as a telesales person, having spent most of the three hours ringing Dial-a-Disc – which just goes to show you how long ago it was – before inventing an imaginary call from an imaginary agent with an imaginary interview for that afternoon. I left at lunchtime and never went back. Several years later, during the mid-eighties, I did some telephone market research for an agency in London. This proved more successful. Calling people from a prescribed list to ask how many BT sockets they had in their house, my most surprising respondent was an elderly woman who told me that she had thirty-five. I questioned the number.

'Thirty-five?' I warbled in my very best Lady Bracknell impersonation. 'Thirty-five? Telephone sockets?'

'Oh no, love! One is for the toaster, one is for the kettle, and my Ladyshave is plugged into one in the...'

I needed no further information. I had a short period in a wine bar in Covent Garden, working as barman and glass collector, a role in which I was officially known as a floor walker. Mercifully I haven't had to resort to street walker – something I would surely have had to do on a sale-or-return basis.

Getting a job to supplement your income, that also allows you freedom for auditions and the occasional one- or two-day television job, can be difficult. Many jobs can provide income at the expense of self-esteem and dignity. You have spent a great deal of time, effort and money on your training, and yet here you are as a shop assistant, or a temp in an office. Good jobs but not the ones you have dreamed of doing. The worst case scenario is that, between each and every acting job, you have to find a new temporary job and start once more at the beginning. Actors who have found alternative work to which they can return are indeed very lucky. 70% of the people who responded to my survey said that they spent less than half their year working as an actor. 48% of those who answered said that they had a job they could return to between acting engagements, ranging from supply teaching to freelance copywriting. 30% said that they had to find a new part-time job each time, and this was the group who had to look for bar work, shop work, and other roles with very little job satisfaction.

Maximising your work opportunities is key. You have acquired a unique set of talents as an actor from your training, and from your experience you have acquired knowledge and ability. These skills may serve you well in making you one of the best shop assistants in the team, and giving you that edge in customer relations. Drama training is probably one of the most useful educations that people can undertake, suitable for so many roles, in life as well as on the stage. However, if your desire is to be an actor, then temporary jobs that use your acting skills in some way are to be preferred.

There is a whole variety of work now available to actors using their skills and offering some very lucrative opportunities, which we commonly refer to as working in the 'corporate sector'. I'm going to declare an interest here. I have been working in the corporate sector for over twenty years alongside my film and television work. At many times it has supported me, and it has certainly guaranteed me a level of income that has made life a great deal easier. It has also provided funds for me to take on low-paid theatre jobs which have fed my soul. My first book, *So You Want To Be A Corporate Actor?*, not only tells you what sort of work there is in the corporate market, but it goes into great detail about how to do it. It looks at events, promotions and how to do role-play, so that when you approach a role-play company and attend an audition, you'll fully understand the process, be more prepared, and hopefully more successful in getting work from them. I fully understand that you may not yet have purchased that book at the bargain price Nick Hern Books are selling it for, so let's take a look at just what the corporate world holds for you.

Role-play

You probably already know an actor who does corporate role-play. It's the area of the corporate market in which most actors work. Used in both training situations and in assessment centres, role-play really started gaining ground in Britain from the mid-eighties. Just a few actors did it and it was quite a specialised way of earning money alongside one's acting. Now there are actors who have made this their sole occupation. They work in nothing but corporate role-play, and they do quite well out of it. They may work for several companies, or training consultants. There are now many business-training companies, and role-play companies who use actors. They vary greatly in quality and in rates of pay. Equity has a role-play agreement, though, by its own admission, this is several years out of date. It is available on their website and it may give you guidance as to the rates of pay currently in operation. Searching for 'role-play companies' online will bring up the main players, as well as several activities for which you need special equipment and rubber garments. Steps are probably the market leaders and employ a huge number of actors each year. React, Roleplay UK, Simpatico UK, Role Call and Interact, are all companies who employ actors.

Like any other employer, you will have to make that cold leap and contact them, but it's good to bear in mind the principles you looked at in writing a letter. All of the leading role-play training companies get a large number of generic applications from actors every day, so you should target the companies in exactly the same way that you would target any other employer. Be specific in what you want.

If you write:

> 'As a talented actor with a large number of credits, I'm currently looking to expand my work opportunities into the role-play industry. Please would you contact me if anything suitable comes up.'

Then this will almost certainly be read as:

> 'As an actor who is currently out of work and desperate, I'm trying to pick up something from role-play, as I know some actors do this. Please give me a job.'

Before you write, do your research. Read up about the company. Find out what their strengths are. Look at the names of the account managers. Who are their clients? Do you know any actors who have worked with them and might recommend you?

You may get a response saying that they have an awful lot of actors on their books at the moment and don't have enough work for them. This will very probably be the case with many of the companies. These are actors, however, who, alongside their role-play work, are still doing film and television work and therefore rendering themselves unavailable for jobs in the corporate market. Every role-play company has a shifting workforce. Sometimes they have accounts that require specific skills, and it's at this point that you, the new role-player, might be immensely useful to them.

Ask the company how they like actors to approach them. Then whatever they say, let that guide your approach. If they do reply saying that they already have an enormous number of actors, respond to them and say 'thank you' for getting back in touch and when would be a good time for you to mail them again?

Don't then delete them from your list. Start a new list of contacts and dates. Make a note of when they suggested that you might get in touch, and follow it up at that point.

Again, establish a dialogue with somebody at the company. Try and verify that this is someone who ultimately does make decisions regarding actors, but treat them with respect.

It's always interesting as to where feedback about actors comes from. When I have been casting a play, it has proved useful to have a friend of mine, or a friendly ASM, to manage the waiting auditionees and usher them into the room. At the end of the day, their feedback about how the actors behaved while they were waiting and chatting to their peers is invaluable. On more than one occasion, someone's behaviour outside an audition room has taken them out of the running for a job.

So from that very first email, treat the person as though they are a decision-maker. They might only be a gatekeeper but, like the doctor's receptionist, you're not going to get an appointment without their help.

Role-play requires you to be very comfortable with improvisation. If you're not, then the role-play world is not for you. You will learn a short brief, and then work with a participant who will not be an actor. They will not be acting, and neither should you. You are there to serve them, so it requires a selfless persona. Many actors don't have this, and that's absolutely fine. You have to be comfortable doing a job where it is all about the other person. So often, as actors, it's about us. Many of the role-play companies run workshop auditions, which are a good test of your suitability for the style of work, as well as your ability to deliver it. Role-play is used in the medical world for the training of doctors' communication skills and breaking bad news. It is used heavily in the business world in situations as diverse as lawyers preparing for legal cases to difficult exit interviews and embarrassing HR situations.

When it is well executed by trained actors, role-play is probably one of the most valuable training methods around, and as such it can pay well. While there still are some cowboy outfits offering actors £50 a day, the reputable role-play companies, such as those I mentioned, tend to offer a minimum daily rate in the region of £200 a day (at the time of writing). Some jobs can pay considerably more. And the added benefit is that you'll be working with people who understand actors. Many role-play companies were set up by actors themselves, so working for them can be a chance to earn some money and yet be among your own tribe!

Live events and promotional work

Live events and promotional work can involve anything from compèring a top-class charity auction to dressing in a foam-rubber Play Doh costume and dancing in the aisles of Toys 'R' Us. Just to point out, no I haven't made that up! Coming into this area of work, it's more likely you'll make contact with the foam rubber than the charity function at first. It's an area of work with an increasing number of companies, and as such it's important that you check out the conditions and standard of work before accepting the job. The big players in this area are KruLive, Mash Staffing, and iD Staffing, and they all draw a lot of their talent base from actors.

What are the skills and talents that you need in order to make this a viable living? I know several young actors who do promotional work every weekend, and on some other days when they have no acting work on, and they're earning enough each month to pay their rent and to live. This means that the rest of their week as a Working Actor is focused on developing skills and getting other work. Just as it should be.

Richard Holborn is a few years out of his training. He's incredibly enterprising and has involved himself in a great number of projects during his first year, many of which have been unpaid. They have paid dividends in that he is now part of a flourishing new agency, and so the investment of his time has been worthwhile, but he still has to support himself financially. Applying for a job with KruLive through a tweet on the Actors Centre Twitter feed, Richard got himself a job. Since that first booking, he has had several more, and the promotional work that Kru are providing has become a key part of his financial support system. I asked him about the world of the promotional event.

What is promotional work and how did you get involved?

I graduated from drama school and, during my studies, I sustained myself with a part-time 'day job', which demanded so much of my energy that I decided that once I had paid my fees I would quit and earn money on acting alone. Cue laughter. That obviously is one of the hardest things to do, although I have been lucky in having some great acting contracts. It's all about finding the balance. It wasn't until June this year that I started to delve into the world of promo. I say delve, but my first job was for a banking flash mob where a hundred of us paraded around Central London and took our kit off. It was executed in a very tasteful way and the pay wasn't bad either.

Sounds quite theatrical?

Sorry, did you think it was just chucking leaflets at people and muttering a few inaudible words off-voice? Well, you are very much mistaken, or I should say... it depends who you work for/with. I work in a freelance capacity. I work for KruLive and KruTalent International, but I know there are other companies doing this sort of work. It has been great because I get to work with other creative professionals and, therefore, I'm networking, sharing and solving problems with like-minded people. I enjoy working directly with clients, and it's nice to work on different campaigns each week. Variety really is the spice of life.

What do you do?

It very much depends on the brief I am booked on. Sometimes I will need to hone my hosting skills at, say, a Wild West event (we had amazing hats), and on another occasion I might need to do some street theatre. Oh, that sounds like acting... well, really, it is. Promo is either for you or not for you, but the skills needed are very much transferable for anyone with a theatrical background. You have to be good at selling – selling yourself to get repeat bookings and selling the product or event. As a Working Actor, you have to see yourself as a business, so this is a vital skill, regardless of whether promo is something you get into.

What's the dollar like?

The pay offers a decent wage, for work that is industry-related. Above National Minimum Wage, and with travel expenses and sometimes catering covered. For me, this type of work has enabled me to keep busy. I cannot highlight how important that is, because it keeps momentum up. It's a hard industry to break into and this has certainly helped.

How?

Well, firstly, a regular income is always handy. I have recently been offered a few acting contracts off of the back of my promo work, which is a great bonus. This in turn has helped with my motivation. I have now secured a great agent, which in turn has enabled me to be seen for more work.

Enthusing oneself on something you might not be passionate about is a challenge, but you have to be passionate to deliver a good job. This is not the job for people who cannot engage easily. Promo work is great for the CV, both your acting CV and that 'regular one'. Good for your acting CV because I've now added other skills to my CV. Skin work, workshops with children, crafts, hosting– stuff that is really helpful, especially when Spotlight briefs are asking more of us. Good for my regular CV because I'm working on various projects, with big brands and exercising lots of different skills needed in all jobs. Not that I plan to work in a nine-to-five job ever again. But keeping this CV full is never a bad thing.

How does it work?

It can be difficult to get your foot in the door. I applied in January and then finally got booked on my first job in June. Apparently that's not a very long time to wait.

How do you book a job?

An average week would involve sending in my availability and checking on the jobs board on the KruLive website to see if anything takes my fancy. You can select the dates you would like to work and put yourself up for the jobs. You will also receive emails from the booking agent – this is where you can get most bookings. If you reply quickly with a detailed but concise email with your relevant experience, you will generally get booked on the job. Promo can be very organised and when it is it's a dream job. Once booked, you will get sent a very simple brief to study over with location details, your role details and who to report to – generally the rule is to follow that and there will be no problems.

On occasion things do go wrong (such is life). The thing to remember, as with the acting... there is no: 'It should have been like this.' Last weekend I was booked as a bellboy for a two-day street-theatre and promo gig. We got on site, and the office with our costumes and basically everything we needed was locked up. We improvised as best we could. But in the end, we rang the office and they were lovely and sent us home on full pay for doing nothing. You are still getting paid, so stay professional and polite, as often your contact at the office has hundreds of people out all at once and might not know the specifics of your brief, especially if it's a weekend job. I've had one or two wrong locations or things missing when you've turned up to work... but you just deal with it, and Kru are always very good about this. Don't be precious either. Promotional work is lots of fun. It just demands lots of energy, clarity, and a little bit of improvisation.

I like to think of all acting work as adventures, I think that's the best way of keeping positive in 'the Machine' that is the industry. With this in mind, promo and corporate work are my days out – it's very social and you really don't feel like you are working. I've been to some fantastic locations and made some great friends on the way.

***

Richard seems to be making it work for him. How can you make it work for you? First you need to choose a company to work for. As I mentioned earlier, KruLive are not the only promotions company out there. Mash and iD are both thought to be on par with Kru – check them out online and see what you think.

Tom Eatenton is the Chief Executive of KruLive, and I'm able to recommend the working process, the recruitment process, and indeed the payment process, of this company wholeheartedly. There is an online directory called www.stuckforstaff.com which gives an extensive list of staffing agencies. I'd strongly advise that you research the recruitment, briefing and pay-ment process prior to registering with any agency.

Registering with Kru is easy. You visit their website (www.krulive.com) and register your details. You will then be invited to a workshop with a group of other potential recruits, where you'll be taken through a series of exercises to assess your suitability for the sort of work that they do.

Tom told me that, in an average year, KruLive use several thousand people on their events. Anything from product launches to flash mobs, from leafleting to computer-game demonstrations. Approximately 60% of those events based in London would be staffed by actors. The face-to-face nature of the work makes people with outgoing, lively and enthusiastic personalities perfect for it. It means they can engage the target client easily and create 'theatre' to make the encounter memorable.

Without a doubt, the major downside to using actors is reliability. This sort of work is obviously perceived as secondary to the primary passion and career of actor. It is understandable, but it's good to remember that life is all about making commitments and keeping them. Far too often actors will agree and commit to a booking, their details and profile cards will be sent on to the end client who will approve their choice and invite them onto the teams. This can sometimes involve cost in training them for the event, only for the actor to pull out on the day due to an audition or interview. KruLive are one of many companies that completely understand the need for actors to audition. They also need to mitigate the damage to their reputation that a last-minute cancellation from an actor can do. Kru works from the premise that, once you have agreed and committed to an activity or an event with them, you need to see it through if you want to be booked regularly. They do their best to replace people so that they can attend important castings, but if that's not possible then they do ask that the actors follow through with the booking as agreed.

People who are reliable, enthusiastic, get on well with the booking team and receive great client feedback will pretty much have their choice of work. There is work for anyone as long as they are reliable. A great personality and an ability to work hard will take you far. Looks are important in this industry, but they aren't everything. Someone with 'model' looks who doesn't want to get their hands dirty and work hard probably won't be asked back. Someone with a great personality, a great work ethic and who is well-presented is always attractive to the public and the brands that Kru represent.

As with any temporary job, you have to decide if this is the sort of work for you. It doesn't necessarily guarantee continuity, and the frequency of the work depends on your ability, but it is an area where there is a lot of work, and much of it can be evening events and weekends. It will call on the most basic of your acting skills, and can quite often be great fun. From improvising in character to dealing with members of the public as a host or guide, the choice can often be yours.

But let's be honest: wearing a slogan-bearing T-shirt and interacting with people at a trade fair, or masquerading as a giant sponge finger in a supermarket, may not be your cup of tea. So let's take a look at another company who pride themselves on using actors as their workforce and make every effort to accommodate their requests.

Call centres

Mercifully, my communication skills have improved since I was calling people and asking them about their telephone sockets, and so has the technology used in call centres. We've all had experience of call centres, whether we have had to call them, or whether they have called us. We might not like them, but we are all capable of recognising the difference between talking to somebody who is good on the line and someone who isn't. RSVP, a London-based call centre, prides itself on having good people on the end of the phone because it specialises in using actors.

'All our team could get a job tomorrow, and we'd have no workforce,' says Stephen Thorne, director of resources at RSVP, an outsourcing call centre run and staffed entirely by actors. Here is the perfect actor-friendly company. They advertise quite openly to their clients that all their telephones are manned by actors, and it's a big selling point. Employers wanting good people on their telephones understand that actors do this well. However, Stephen acknowledges that this has to be a two-way process, and in order to reap the benefits of a thespian workforce, they have to be actor-friendly too. So here is a company who are quite happy to give you time off for auditions, even at very short notice. All they ask is that you have an email from your agent, or from the company giving you the audition, to verify the appointment.

There's a huge buzz when you enter the office in London's Docklands. On the day I went to find out just how RSVP copes with all these actors in one room, reception was full of people filling out application forms, and the phone team were working hard.

You can apply to RSVP by visiting their website (www.rsvp.co.uk) and completing an online form. They have regular interview days and you'll be invited along to the next one.

'You don't need to be a rocket scientist or have any specialised sales knowledge,' says Stephen. 'You just need to be able to absorb, to engage, to improvise, and to work from a script, which hopefully, as an actor, are all things that have been part of your training.'

If RSVP like you at the interview, you will then be invited along to train. Training takes three days, for which you are paid, and this is the only time that RSVP would expect you to commit and attend fully. After training you'll be placed onto a phone team on a variety of projects. Due to the current state of the market, most of the work is currently sales, and you can find yourself selling anything from magazine subscriptions to fine wine. You don't have to be the most amazing salesperson – in fact, if you are a brilliant salesperson, then RSVP may not be the place for you, as it's certainly not going to make you a millionaire. Basic rates including low commission can start at around £8.50 an hour, and good sellers, I'm told, can easily earn £12.50 an hour. If sales don't work for you, then there are some customer service roles, which can involve taking people through a telephone questionnaire, and follow-up calls on home services, although this might not guarantee you as many shifts.

RSVP prefer you to work at least four shifts a week, but you can work as many as you want and are able to. They acknowledge the need of actors doing casual work to be paid quickly, so the shifts you work in one week will be paid at the end of the next week. No hanging about till the end of the month, and given that this is a company that employs a huge number of actors, they understand tax and how actors need to be paid.

At RSVP you would be working with a company that understands you as an actor, and needs you. They know they are number two in your working priorities. 'Hopefully a close number two,' says Stephen, 'but we understand that the acting will always come first.' Stephen also told me that they do take an interest in the welfare and the careers of their team. They understand that you are not a call-centre agent, but that at heart you are an actor. They know that a mix of the two will help you produce the best results for them, and will keep you happy. To this end, RSVP has links with several industry partners, and hosts open days for headshot photographers, showreel producers, all of whom provide RSVP staff discounts and offers. Stephen understands actors – but then that shouldn't be a surprise, as he was one for many years. He worked at RSVP alongside his acting work for seventeen years, recently having made the change from actor to full-time director of resources. The great thing about him, though, is his passion for what actors do when they're not working in the call centre. Support like this is hard to find. To many employers, the fact that you might have to rush off for an audition is a reason not to employ you. RSVP turn your status as an actor into an asset.

RSVP's main demographic in its workforce are young recent graduates, although it is open to applications from actors of all ages. The work can be exacting, but you will be among your tribe, fellow actors who understand you. Quite often, one of the downsides of being out of work or doing temporary jobs is that you miss the company of other actors. But at RSVP you will find that in abundance, so although you might not actually be acting, you will still feel as though you're in the swing of things, and the news and gossip that a group of actors generates can be incredibly useful for you in terms of work contacts.

***

Of course, there are many opportunities for work to fill in the gaps between your acting jobs. This is by no means meant to be an exhaustive list, just a guide to help you find something interesting and hopefully rewarding. But let's be honest about it here. Your gaps may well be longer than your career. Equity statistics on how many days a year an actor works do not make for happy reading. So it makes sense to try and find a secondary job that can bring a sense of fulfilment, and an ability to use your skill set. Yes, there are jobs in shops and jobs in pubs. You can wait on tables, or you can use some of your existing skills. I can count among my acquaintance actors who run Zumba classes, who teach at drama schools and who work as freelance copywriters and proofreaders. In my survey, 48% of the actors who responded said that they had a secondary job that they could return to. Do you? Many actors reaching their late twenties take time out to gather a qualification to ensure this continuity – Teaching English as a Foreign Language (TEFL), a fast-track teaching course so that they can work as a supply teacher. All these are good backups, but first and foremost you want to remain as a Working Actor. This is a major consideration to be taken when choosing that second job.

Work Task

Make a list of role-play companies that you might like to investigate. Write to some of them to see if they have any training sessions coming up that you might be able to join.

If you feel that promotional work might be for you, then visit www.krulive.com or www.stuckforstaff.com, and check out some of the other promotional agencies.

Visit www.rsvp.co.uk and learn a little more about how they operate. If it's for you, then drop them a line.

If you're a Spotlight member, then it's worth checking out www.spotlight.com/offers/nonacting, where a whole list of non-acting work can be found. Ranging from call-centre work to manning stalls in Camden market. Well worth a look.

Shameless book-promoting work task

Go online to www.nickhernbooks.co.uk and order a copy of my other book, *So You Want To Be A Corporate Actor?* It not only gives you leads to companies who use actors in the corporate sector, but it contains a comprehensive guide as to how to perform role-play well, and just what you can expect working on live events, promotional stunts, and other activities in the corporate world. People have said it's quite funny too!

19. Working – and playing

Actors enjoy being with other people. It's an essential part of the work. Being in a group of people and creating something together. The job demands that you interact well. The sort of friendship that can take other people weeks to establish can be built between working actors in a few hours. I heard Alison Steadman telling the well-known adage that you could meet an actor on set and end up in bed with them an hour later. I think she was talking about in front of the camera, though I'm sure there have been occasions when other interpretations of that instant friendship have happened. Whatever the result, actors do thrive in the company of other actors.

When the work isn't there, being with your tribe can be one of the first things you miss. Being with the people who understand how you work, and what you do when you work. Sometimes it's necessary to get away from other actors, to clear the mind of all things theatrical and dramatic. The actor Alex Jennings told me that the reason he went to Warwick University before he went to drama school was that he wanted to spend time with people who didn't want to be actors – probably a good choice at the age of eighteen. Widening the social circle of people you know can only enrich your work.

Ultimately, however, the Working Actor wants to spend time with other actors. You will have many friends who are actors, and they will be your primary support network. Sometimes the very fact that they are friends can make it hard to talk to them about work when you don't have any, and they do. Great friendships forged at drama school can often fall apart within months when one person is successful in obtaining work, and the other can't get a foothold in the business. Suddenly the one thing you had in common is taken away, and the friendship can struggle.

Up until the early eighties, as an unemployed actor, you could choose where you signed on for unemployment benefit, and many actors from all over London would choose to sign on at Chadwick Street Employment Exchange in Westminster. It became an unofficial meeting place for actors, and the cafés around there were full of us, exchanging job information, tales of woe and gossip of the most salacious kind – and perhaps cashing in on the Alison Steadman school of friendship! Sadly now there isn't one particular branch of Starbucks or Costa Coffee that is inhabited by the acting profession and, as a younger actor, it can be hard to find a place where you have the opportunity to chat to actors of all ages, find out what is going on, and to work alongside people to hone your skills and prepare for work. Actors needing to spend time with other actors was the core reason behind the establishment of the Actors Centre in 1978. The actors Clive Swift, Sheila Hancock, John Alderton, and the fight director William Hobbs, had a vision of creating a place where actors could network and support each other.

That is exactly what the Actors Centre provides. Having had temporary homes at the YMCA on Tottenham

Court Road, where workshops were led by Sir Ian McKellen, and then renting premises in Dryden Street and Chenies Street, the Actors Centre finally purchased 1a Tower Street, a former industrial building in the heart of Covent Garden. It's been transformed over the years into a creative hub serving a growing community of actors. With an eighty-seat theatre, the Tristan Bates Theatre, four rehearsal studios and a vocal studio, editing and self-taping facilities, and a green room and café, it provides a central haven for actors of all generations. Patrons have included Olivier, Julie Walters, Alan Bates, Rafe Spall, David Harewood and Joely Richardson. The aim of the Actors Centre is to support actors in their work; to offer a bridge between unemployment and the world of work; to provide opportunities to learn new skills and to extend existing ones; to meet new people and to learn from other Working Actors.

There is an ever-changing and comprehensive programme of workshops, ranging from one-to-one audition-speech coaching, screen-work classes and Meisner technique sessions, to an Actors Centre choir, quiz nights, networking events and quite a few good parties. As a member you have access to a whole range of free events, such as lunchtime chat shows and Q&A sessions with top casting directors; discounts on tickets at the Tristan Bates; a range of goods and services, such as gym membership, photographs, theatre books, etc. – as well as somewhere to meet up with people or simply hang about and have a coffee in the centre of town when you have some time to kill.

Of course, all this doesn't come free. Membership at the very top end costs around £75 a year. There are considerable discounts for people joining in the first couple of years out of drama school, and there are reductions for existing members who renew their membership early. You can take out a six-month membership, or save money and enrol for a year. There are entrance criteria to becoming a member of the Actors Centre that prevent people from just walking in off the street and taking advantage of the resources. You have to have completed an accredited course at a UK drama school (see www.actorscentre.co.uk if you're unsure), have Equity or Spotlight membership, or have at least four evidential and verifiable professional acting credits. These criteria mean that you as a member will be meeting and working alongside people who are as serious about their work as you are.

At this point I have to confess an interest. In 2008 I was asked to join the Board of the Actors Centre, to provide some guidance and help as to how actors might work in the corporate sector. I was intrigued by the invitation and eventually persuaded to say yes. My impressions of the Actors Centre at that point were none too positive. I viewed it as a place that was only used by actors who are out of work and couldn't find any. Actors who were acting simply for their own sake rather than really making a living out of it. Often we are told that the downfall of the English actor is that we don't want to take classes. American actors are good at taking classes; in fact, some American actors are so good at taking classes that that's all they ever do. They don't really act. They spend their life as waiters or cab drivers and then they take a class. As an English actor who has completed three years of rigorous professional training, and a training that is still acknowledged as the best in the world, the last thing you probably want to do upon leaving drama school is go and take a class. Yet you will acknowledge that there are gaps in your learning. You may not have done as much screen work as you would have liked during your time at drama school or in the first few years of your career. The more time you spend in front of the camera, the more comfortable you become. You may not have met many of the major casting directors, and the thought of having to go into an interview with one of them may fill you with dread. All of these problems can be remedied in workshops at the Actors Centre.

Since joining the Board, my perception of the organisation has changed, and indeed now, as Chairman of the Board, I would like to think that the organisation itself has changed. I now know that the Actors Centre is not here just for people to play at acting. It's here to help actors sustain and enhance a career. That's what it does best, and hopefully that's what it can continue to do for a long time to come.

Of course, the Actors Centre is not the only organisation that does this. The fact that the Actors Centre has a planned curriculum with workshops advertised up to three months in advance was one of the very reasons that prompted a group of actors to form The Actors' Guild: they wanted more control over the workshops that were offered. Founded in December 2010, The Actors' Guild, like the Actors Centre, became a not-for-profit organisation focused on supporting and empowering actors.

The most significant difference between the two organisations, who both seem to have a common purpose in mind, is that The Actors' Guild is nomadic; it is not building-based. Members can post on the website and request workshops, and as soon as enough members have requested the workshop, that workshop will be provided. The Actors' Guild use a variety of venues, from the Spotlight offices in Leicester Square, to rehearsal rooms and facilities around London and the rest of the UK. Editing classes can be held in editing suites. Horse-riding for actors can be held on the gallop in Warwickshire. Given that there is no building to support, the membership fees of The Actors' Guild are lower than that of the Actors Centre – at the time of writing around £24 (but there are fewer free events and individual workshops can cost more).

Both organisations offer a variety of perks and discounts, so that you can often save the price of your subscription just by taking advantage of some of their offers.

You won't find it hard to find workshops for actors these days, some of them more worthy than others. Many acting, casting and directing workshops are run as purely commercial enterprises. Both the Actors Centre and The Actors' Guild are running workshops in an ethical and not-for-profit way. They're running them for you.

I'm immensely proud of being the Chairman of the Board of the Actors Centre, and I can now see, often at close quarters, just how supportive the organisation is. Researching this it was great to chat to Ben Warren from The Actors' Guild, equally passionate about what his organisation does. There is no reason the two organisations can't work together, and create something very positive out of where they overlap.

Essentially both these organisations are doing the same thing, and both are doing it with style and energy. By using the many opportunities they provide, you can increase your skill set and your network. And those are the sorts of things that lead to work.

Work Task

So the first thing on this work task is to check out both these organisations' websites (www.theactorscentre.co.uk and www.theactorsguild.co.uk).

Take a look at their programmes and make a note of workshops that you would like to do in the next month if money were no object.

Have a look at the discounts and perks page of each organisation. Are you thinking of getting your headshots done in the near future? Do they offer a photographer you like at a discounted price?

Think about the benefits of having an actual place in Central London that you can pop into for a coffee and which is, in essence, 'your club'. The Actors Centre can provide this.

Think about the workshop that you want to do that isn't listed on either of the sites, and send an email to The Actors' Guild or to the team at the Actors Centre to see if it is something that they're planning.

20. Networking for work

If someone told me I had to network in order to get work, I'm not sure I'd know where to begin. I know that I could attend lots of press nights, which would make a severe dent in my bank balance and success would depend entirely on who was there. Seeing people can jog memories. Casting directors don't deliberately forget you; you may just have gone off the radar for a little while. I remember in the mid-nineties having to cast a game-show pilot I was directing for Channel 4. Despite having looked in Spotlight for hours on end, I couldn't come up with the right casting for a young man who could disguise himself as a woman to take part in a heist in an East End pub. The actor had to be first-class at improvisation as he would be interrogated by a real detective, an ex-Great Train Robber, and a crime novelist as part of the show. With my mind a little desperate and overwrought, I sat down on the Sunday evening to watch *A Touch of Frost* and suddenly there was my answer. The actor Marc Warren was playing some mysterious killer on a motorbike. I knew Marc a little already and had absolutely no doubt of his ability. He had not been in my thoughts for casting this job. Two phone calls later and he was booked.

So getting out and about and being seen is crucial. But just how do you do that if you're not appearing in an episode of ITV Sunday-night detective drama?

One answer has recently appeared as a new support organisation for actors: The So & So Arts Club. It is a fantastic new venture started from scratch by the actress Sarah Berger, an actress who has had a long and illustrious career encompassing everything from seasons at the RSC to long-running television series. Despite a huge list of great credits, work became harder to find, and the one thing that Sarah isn't is someone who just sits around waiting for opportunity to knock on the door. Having shared a house with her during a Stratford season, watched her play Olivia in *Twelfth Night* with a twisted ankle, and rescued her from a bath of rubble in our house after low-flying aircraft brought the bathroom ceiling down on her, I can vouch wholeheartedly for her tenacity.

The So & So Arts Club is aimed at all actors. Wherever they live. Whatever their age. Launched in June 2012, it originally began as a virtual networking opportunity, a website where members could log in and view casting information, fringe-theatre offers, and any general request they wanted. Its aim was to get actors talking to each other, hoping they might create projects and work.

Membership costs £30 a year, which is highly competitive. This goes towards maintaining the website and funding the many real-world events that the club now promotes and creates. From starting out as a virtual networking opportunity, The So & So Arts Club has become a very real provider of work for actors. In 2014 it staged a repertory season of new plays at Park Theatre in Finsbury Park. The plays staged had all been originally presented as rehearsed readings by the club, and all the casting was from club members. The season was a great critical success, and underlined the need that Sarah had felt was so prevalent when creating the organisation.

The club now has a real bricks-and-mortar base in Frederick Place in the City of London. A building which provides rehearsal space, and a place for club members to meet. The club stages rehearsed readings of new plays and provides great opportunities for actors to get together and try out new work. The great principle behind the club is Sarah's insistence that work means pay. In the first eighteen months of the club, it staged eighteen paid rehearsed readings, took a show to New York, staged several fringe shows, and developed work from its rehearsed readings into full-scale productions in repertory. It has staged a second very successful rep season at Frederick Place, with one production moving to the King's Head for a very successful run.

I asked Sarah why a young actor, with limited resources, should become a member.

'One of the hardest things, I think, for people leaving drama school is that you leave on the crest of a wave. You've got no idea that you've been doing more acting than you're ever going to do in the rest of your life because it's continual. A year down the line, if you've hit the ground running, you've had a few jobs and then you're sitting in your bedsit looking at the wall thinking: "I don't know what to do next because I don't know how to get through the next door. I don't even know where the next door is."'

One thing that The So & So Arts Club aims to do is encourage the gatekeepers of our profession – the agents, the casting directors – to join in with everybody else. To build direct connections; to collaborate rather than leave actors standing outside with their face pressed to the window, constantly looking at everybody on the inside having the time of their lives. The club also provides great opportunities for work and for people to flex their acting muscles. Sarah again:

> 'The other thing I would say to any young actors is to take every opportunity that comes along. One thing we do are rehearsed readings, which are good because you get to meet and work with directors you might otherwise never get into a room with. You're dealing with new writing and new work, and there is a huge interest in that across the industry. Actors need to act. You need to keep practising what you do all the time. You need to go to the acting gym as often as possible, and that involves taking class. It's very American. We don't tend to do it.'

The So & So Arts Club is trying to be much more wide-reaching than the other organisations mentioned here. Much more of its content is generated by members. It means that the range of workshops offered is not as diverse as what you may find at the Actors Centre or The Actors' Guild. The whole nature of the club is that it's much more peripatetic. It's a unique adventure and it's one that is very easy to join as a member. A quick look on their website as I write this and, as a member, I'm offered tickets, five casting requests, ranging from fringe shows to student films, some paid-work opportunities, production information, and two masterclass invitations. Not bad for my £30 a year.

The increased popularity of the club and its resounding success means that now there is much more competition for the casting opportunities it provides, for its readings and its repertory seasons. All of its work is cast from its members, and more members means fewer opportunities. The great thing about it is that, as a member, you have a voice. As far as I can see, the more organisations that exist like this, the better. What Sarah Berger has done here is use her own vast experience and turned it into a magnificent opportunity for many people. For that alone, I have nothing but admiration for her.

Work Task

Visit The So & So Arts Club website (www.thesoand-soartsclub.com). Have a good click around on the site to discover the benefits, and look through the profiles of existing members, and I'm sure you'll find people you know. Chat to them. What do they get out of the club? How have they found it? Is it value for money? You can also take a look at the club's Facebook page, which gives you a great insight into what is going on at the moment. From there you can email Sarah if you have any more questions, but I think it's a great and very worthwhile £30 investment. Particularly good for actors who are feeling a little bit out of the swing of things, and who would like to meet more people.

There is a proliferation of workshops and actor-support organisations increasingly popping up on any online search, and I haven't written about them all here. The reason being that the three I have talked about at length are organisations of which I have personal experience, and understand a little of their benefits and their pitfalls.

I believe them to be worthwhile organisations who are using their best endeavours to support actors at all stages of their careers. Lots of people see actors, particularly young ones, as an opportunity to make money; to turn their dreams into profit for other people. Before you sign up for any acting course, or acting coaching, make sure you find someone who has done it previously and talk to them. Online recommendations are not always what they seem. A little time spent talking to an actor you know and respect about what they got from the course will ensure the workshop brings rich rewards.

21. Getting financial support

When I started acting in the late 1970s, I was lucky enough that the state welfare system acted as a safeguard for my periods out of work. It was hardly questioned by young actors leaving drama school in those days that we would sign on and exist on unemployment benefit while waiting for a job – a sort of government subsidy of the arts. These days the situation is incredibly different. Unemployment benefit claims are time-limited, and after a short period of time you can be asked to attend interviews for jobs not of your choice. You can be asked to retrain, which is hard for anyone who has only recently emerged into the world of work.

I declared myself self-employed in 1998 and haven't claimed any sort of benefit ever since. At times it's been hard, but it has pushed me forward to find work in all sorts and at all times. An important part of allowing yourself to become a Working Actor is allowing yourself time to breathe, and there are times when the benefits system can do this for you. I'm a great believer in the mantra that busy hands are happy hands, and the ability to find a job that uses your skills and provides you with financial support during the periods when you're not acting is far more worthwhile to you as a person than to try and subsist on measly state benefits. But benefits can underpin your financial situation. In many instances they are an entitlement, and while they remain so, I think they should be claimed. The whole benefit scenario is a nightmare to negotiate, and one where I would certainly need specialist advice. I asked Alan Lean, the benefits and tax specialist at Equity, to describe the minefield that is the benefit system. He was immeasurably helpful and went into great detail on the subject. For Equity members, he is at the end of a phone, but for those of you who may not be, here are the broad outlines of the situation that deals with actors.

The business of claiming welfare benefit is something that is becoming increasingly fraught with difficulty in a changing welfare-reform landscape – nonetheless state benefits can still operate as a valuable safety net for actors during periods of low work activity. This is a broad view of the type of benefits that can be claimed, some of the issues involved in claiming them, and some future changes in the pipeline.

A key benefit for actors is Jobseeker's Allowance (JSA) which exists in two forms: contribution-based (CBJSA) and income-based (IBJSA). This is a benefit for those either not working or working less than sixteen hours per week. The contribution-based version, as the name suggests, is dependent on having paid sufficient Class 1 National Insurance contributions (NICs) in the two tax years prior to the year of claim; so, if you were to claim in January 2016, you would be assessed on tax years 2013/2014 and 2014/2015.

Until 6th April 2014, many actors were paying Class 1 NICs on Equity contracts or similar, and so were accumulating entitlement to CBJSA. As from 6th April 2014 actors are now liable to pay Class 2 and Class 4 NICs on those contracts. This results in a loss of entitlement to CBJSA and thereafter you would not qualify unless you have a separate PAYE job, paying sufficient in Class 1s.

It is important to appreciate that, even if you have sufficient National Insurance contributions, the Department for Work and Pensions (DWP) would still need to assess your self-employed income, but with CBJSA it is only your earnings that are taken into account – savings are ignored. If you are claiming IBJSA, any other income from your household needs to be taken into account, e.g. income of a spouse or partner, which may prevent you getting any benefit. Any payments received for work during a claim should be notified to the Jobcentre, and when signing on actors should tell the DWP about any work in the pipeline. This helps to avoid benefit suspensions or overpayments.

When you sign on at a Jobcentre you need to sign a Jobseeker's Agreement. You would certainly want acting to be the principal activity on your work search. You should be allowed to look for this kind of work for the first three months of your claim. Following this, the DWP can insist that you add at least two other work-search activities. You can argue that at least one of these should be related to acting or compatible with going to auditions and other such activities. Those who stay on JSA for a period in excess of three months may find that they are asked to undertake training courses or mandatory work activities.

Following a recent case, any claimant sent on one of these Back to Work schemes should have received sufficient information about the objectives of the scheme, who it is aimed at and what alternative schemes are available. Failure to provide this information could make participation in such a scheme ineffective. If you think you need to challenge your participation in such a scheme, you should seek advice. This is where Equity can be one great source of help, as failure to participate in the scheme may result in non-payment of benefit.

Another benefit that many actors have claimed historically is housing benefit – at present, this can be claimed without also having to claim Jobseeker's Allowance, although this option will disappear when Universal Credit comes in (see below). Housing Benefit can be claimed if you are working and on a low income. The level of benefit can vary greatly as it will be based on the local authority's assessment of market rent for where you live. Thus you need to bear in mind that there may be a considerable shortfall in what Housing Benefit will cover. If you receive income-based Jobseeker's Allowance, then no income assessment is necessary for Housing Benefit.

Both JSA and Housing Benefit should look at your net profit from acting work, but you need to remember that certain expenses will not be allowable as they would be under the tax system – particularly items such as capital expenditure and depreciation. Make sure when claiming benefits that the DWP are using your net profit figures.

When you claim Housing Benefit, you should also claim under your local council's Council Tax Reduction scheme. These schemes have replaced Council Tax Benefit and the details vary from one council to another.

You should look on your local council's website to find details of their scheme and how to claim.

Another benefit actors can claim when working is Working Tax Credit (WTC) – a means-tested and tax-free payment for those in relatively low-paid work. You qualify if you are twenty-five or over and working thirty or more hours a week; alternatively, you need to be at least sixteen years old and working sixteen or more hours per week, with either a dependent child or a disability, or you are aged sixty-plus. The main problem from the actor's perspective is the thirty-hour requirement, although you can include the time you spend on activities necessary to your self-employment, such as bookkeeping and research work. A further complication is that you may find HMRC looking further into your claim if they think you are not running your business on a commercial basis, e.g. if your average hourly profit from your self-employment is less than the National Minimum Wage if you are under 25 (£6.70 per hour from October 2015)/National Living Wage for over-25s (£7.20 per hour from April 2016). Nonetheless, it may be worth claiming WTC during, for example, a theatre run which is relatively low-paid.

It is important to appreciate that state benefits are available to the self-employed when you are sick. The main benefit, which replaced Incapacity Benefit, is Employment Support Allowance. It is limited to a twelve-month period. For the first thirteen weeks, your claim can be supported by a medical certificate. After that you would need a medical exam to continue to claim. There are often huge backlogs with these medicals, currently carried out by an outsourced private sector company called Maximus.

One other benefit worth mentioning is Maternity Allowance, which can be claimed by self-employed workers who are expecting a child – it can be claimed for a period of up to thirty-nine weeks at any time from eleven weeks before the expected date of childbirth.

On the horizon looms Universal Credit, the brainchild of Iain Duncan Smith (gone but not missed), which is currently well behind schedule in its implementation. It appears that the self-employed will be fully included from 2017. This represents a highly significant reform to the welfare system, in that one benefit will replace a whole series of means-tested benefits – Child Tax Credit, Working Tax Credit, Housing Benefit, IRESA, IBJSA and Income Support. Universal Credit will incorporate elements which previously represented separate benefits, e.g. a housing element, children element, and so on. There will be greater flexibility in terms of hours worked and more generous income disregards (amounts of earnings ignored before impacting on benefits received), and for some actors it will provide a valuable support even during periods of work. Contribution-based benefits such as CBJSA or CBESA will continue and are not affected by Universal Credit.

Despite the fact that there are some positive features of Universal Credit, at the time of writing there are two in particular that are causing concern not just for actors but also for other self-employed groups – something called the Minimum Income Floor and the concept of 'gainful self-employment'. Both of these are highly problematic for the self-employed – the Minimum Income Floor assumes a level of earnings from self-employment, in a straightforward case, equal to the National Minimum Wage multiplied by 35, which would equate, as from October 2015, to an annual figure of £11,830.

Any award would therefore assume this level of income as a minimum, irrespective of your actual income. This floor applies if you are viewed as 'gainfully self-employed', i.e. carrying on a trade, profession or vocation as your main employment which is 'organised, developed and regular and carried on in expectation of profit' and the earnings obtained are self-employed earnings. Situations may occur where actors are viewed as self-employed but assumed to have more income than they actually do, or are not viewed as gainfully self-employed and consequently may be coerced into looking for any full-time work and heavily sanctioned if they fail to comply.

Equity is in ongoing discussions with the DWP and is working with other stakeholders to try and ensure that the new Universal Credit rules will be applied fairly and intelligently to its members.

It is important for actors to realise that there are mechanisms available to challenge DWP decisions – if you request that a decision be looked at again, there is now a new system which applies to many benefits. This results in the DWP issuing a decision on your claim, and Equity have noted a sharp drop in appeals following such reconsiderations. It is therefore very important to seek advice when problems with benefits, or decisions which you consider to be incorrect, occur.

For Equity members, Equity runs an Advice and Rights Helpline, which gives advice on tax, National Insurance and welfare-benefits issues. This is open on Mondays and Thursdays from 10:00–13:00 and 14:00–17:00 on 020 7670 0223, or you can email helplineenquiries@equity.org.uk.

General information on all the benefits mentioned above can be found at the following links:

- https://www.gov.uk/browse/benefits/jobseekers-allowance

- https://www.gov.uk/browse/benefits/families

- https://www.gov.uk/browse/benefits/tax-credits

- https://www.gov.uk/housing-benefit/overview

I'm incredibly grateful to Alan for such a comprehensive overview of what is available. This also gives a really practical example of the benefits of joining Equity.

Work Task

You will know your own financial situation better than anyone else, but are there any benefits you are eligible for which might provide support and for which you are not currently claiming?

Housing Benefit can provide much-needed support for people who are working in less than full-time jobs.

Little disclaimer: all figures are correct as of October 2015, but please check current rates and limits.

22. Using social media

When I started work as an actor in 1978, the main opportunity for networking was your agent's Christmas party. As many casting directors as your agent could pour free wine down would be gathered in one room, and the agency staff would shift you from one to another as often as they could manage until the alcohol began to take hold. If you were featuring in a major role on television, your agent might think it worth investing in some printed cards with your photograph and a still from the series, together with transmission details, and the cards would be dutifully mailed, most probably second class, to as many casting directors and producers as your agent felt they could manage. And that was what passed for 'Getting Your Name Out There'.

Today the power to publicise your face, name and abilities has now been placed in your own hands. The really good agents will all have news pages on their websites listing what their clients are up to, and they will most probably have a Twitter account to announce who will be appearing on television, on stage, and when. This is nothing that you can't do yourself, and many agents actively encourage clients to do as much self-promotion as they can. It's a good way to notify an awful lot of people as to what you're up to, and if a casting director sees a tweet from you, and one from your agent, then there is perhaps a slightly greater chance that they'll watch you.

When Twitter and Facebook became part of our lives, probably very few of us realised how big a part they would come to play in our work, considering they started out as a novelty way of exchanging holiday snaps, views on modern life and our day-to-day existence. 'Went out last night. Got totally blathered. Hungover' is the sort of Facebook status that has prompted me to hit the 'unfriend' button on many occasions. That is entirely a personal opinion. I have Twitter and Facebook accounts and enjoy them both, but it's incredibly important to realise that these can figure in your life as a Working Actor, sometimes without you realising it.

Facebook for me is about friends, though admittedly it has devalued the word. Someone who formerly might have been an acquaintance or someone with whom you have had only the most fleeting of meetings now has access to your photographs and your innermost thoughts. So do people who may be thinking of employing you, people who watch you at the theatre or on television, and people who quite simply Google you, if you do not have your privacy settings correctly adjusted. I make a distinction between Twitter and Facebook as work and play respectively: my Facebook account is for my (actual) friends, and so I have adjusted my privacy settings to reflect that. It's not absolutely failsafe and sometimes people can click through from one of my contacts, but they will get the minimum of information about me, such as date of birth, school, where I live and my partner. They won't be able to click through the rest of my life as displayed in status updates and photographs. I try and ensure that information contained on my Facebook account is limited to private life. As such, I want to limit the people who can see that. You can set up a Facebook group or fan page which can be used as a contact point with the outside world. If you limit its content to work-related photographs, and refrain from status updates on your alcohol level, it can be a useful tool for people searching for you.

Twitter is another ballgame entirely. The best piece of advice I've ever been given about tweeting is not to tweet anything that you wouldn't stand at your front door and shout. Personally, there are a lot of things I am not afraid of shouting, but I think it's a really good thought to have in mind when you broadcast your thoughts. Lots of people use Twitter to tell the world what they're doing, and that's why people follow you: to find out what you're up to. A short stint in the Channel 4 soap *Hollyoaks* produced a surge in my Twitter followers from a somewhat dubious demographic, but all wanting to find out more about me as they thought they knew me from television. And, of course, they do. You are in their living rooms. You are in their private space, and they want and expect to get to know you. You can block followers on Twitter, but given that its main purpose is as a noticeboard where you can post your views, opinions and your news, the more people you have circulating that information on your behalf, the better. That means that you have to restrict your tweets to the information you don't mind people knowing about you. Do your fans and prospective employers really need to know that you're not having a very good day? Do people need to know just how 'pissed off' you are that you didn't get that job? Even as an actor who works hard every day at getting work, or while working, it's easy to believe that someone is on a greener side of the field than you are. I would like to think of myself as a generous person, but for years a little bit of me would die inside whenever a friend told me about a job they had got. I might have been totally unsuitable for that job, I might never have been seen for that job, but I was still jealous and envious – I didn't have a job and they did. Luckily, though, at the time they told me they were probably buying me a pint. People who flag up their success on your Twitter stream don't have to be so generous. They can announce their joy wholeheartedly and you just have to cope with it.

Twitter can be some people's way of dealing with the fact that things aren't going as well as they might want them to. The fervent belief that if they put out a successful image to the world, then that is what the world will believe, is sometimes hard to disagree with. Yet it can be irritating. An actor who I used to follow on Twitter tweets at least twenty or thirty times a day. Each tweet is about work. About their blog. About some film they are appearing in. About what a good life they have as an actor. At times it becomes incredibly irritating. This actor mainly does unpaid films, doesn't have an agent, and creates an awful lot of unpaid work for themselves. None of those things are bad in themselves, indeed, it's what I have espoused in this book about getting out there and doing things. They are tweeting an image of success. (To a rather annoying level, it has to be admitted.) I'm known to tweet pics when I'm doing work. A 140-character comment about the state of my trailer or, if it's allowed, a quick photo in costume. It all looks pretty good. But I don't tweet about the interviews and meetings that don't go so well.

I don't tweet about the days when I sit at home and it's a real struggle to make myself do something. That's all private and personal, and that's how I intend to keep it. So it's worth bearing in mind that what you get on a Twitter feed is probably not everything that's happening in people's lives. When you're sitting at home reading it, however, these positive perky musings of others can be depressing. It's what some people call their 'front stage'. It's their show for the world. It's the highlights, just as hopefully you are tweeting the good things that are happening to you... in moderation.

So it's good to get definition between what you use Facebook for and what you hope to achieve on Twitter. Remember, many contracts prevent you from publishing images or information about projects that you're involved in on social media. The press office of a programme such as *Hollyoaks* or *Coronation Street* will definitely be monitoring comments made about them, and sometimes a quick snap or selfie, or an ill-considered comment, can land you in deep water and ultimately in contractual problems. Chatting on Twitter with a fellow cast member of a soap late one night, I unintentionally revealed my character's forthcoming demise to the world. I was lucky. He pointed it out and I was able to delete the tweet immediately. So always check first, and don't just check with other actors. Ask the people who know, such as the production coordinator, or your agent, or a line producer. Social media is great for getting information out there but there are instances, too numerous to mention, of people getting into serious trouble by tweeting, or updating their status while filming something that the production company has spent a great deal of money on and doesn't want revealed to the public until they are ready.

You can, of course, use a hashtag to join in Twitter conversations about television programmes or plays you have seen and liked, and quite often these comments will be followed by the actors in that programme. I wouldn't be so naive as to suggest that this is a simple way of networking, but it is a way of letting other people know what you thought of their work, and gives actors a chance to appreciate just what their audiences think.

Twitter is also good for the ability to follow people and find out what they're up to. Many casting directors have Twitter feeds. Catherine Willis, the independent casting director who features earlier in this book, has a Twitter feed which she keeps updated with useful information. Don't use Twitter to message casting directors, no matter how appropriate you think it would be. Keep the contact professional. Remember Twitter is like shouting in the street, and you wouldn't shout 'Give us a job!' in the street. Well, I suppose you might, but it would make you look pretty desperate.

And finally do make sure that that your Twitter handle is something appropriate. If you are using Twitter in any professional context, then it should be your name or some very close variation of it. @Furryknickers or @Rotherhamtopcat may all look really good, but just think how you might feel when somebody who is thinking of employing you looks on Twitter and finds that your handle is @Currentloser. I say no more.

Work Task

If you haven't got a Twitter account, why not investigate what is going on. It costs nothing to set up an account, and you could click on some people you're interested in and might like to follow in the work field. Search for their names, or look on their websites and find out if they are on Twitter. You can just follow people without posting any content yourself, and see if you like the process. It certainly can help as a constantly updated noticeboard to get your profile out there just that little bit more.

Take a look at your Facebook settings. Do they let the world see everything? Do you want that? If not, then adjust them to Friends Only. You can do this in the privacy settings in your account.

23. Working with an accountant

When you made that decision to be an actor I'm sure you gave little thought to accountancy. Yet a vital part of a Working Actor's life concerns all matters financial. It's incredibly easy to let these things get out of control. One minute you're earning very little doing a part-time job that you don't particularly like, and then suddenly you do a television series or film, a long run in the West End or a reasonably well-paid commercial, and you find yourself in possession of what might be regarded as a reasonably regular income. Ensuring that the government don't get their hands on too much of this money means filling out a tax return, claiming your expenses, and generally managing your finances in a professional way. So just how do you do it?

You may have already identified the need for an accountant. I know that I did. My parents ran a small corner shop in a Yorkshire mining village, so they had an accountant. He took me on for the first two years of my working life as an actor. He was just a small-town accountant, not a specialist in the world of entertainment, and as a result, I'm afraid, ultimately I had poor guidance. I ended up paying a lot of tax in my first eighteen months as an actor. Tax that should have been defrayed by expenses. He claimed some pretty standard things, but not enough, and it took me several years to recover from those early tax bills. One of the first things I acknowledged was that I am no good with money, and I needed someone to ensure that I didn't get into this amount of trouble again, so I took on an accountant recommended to me by another actor. He was good, and he saved me an awful lot of money over the years, and his death a few years ago was a sad day indeed. Out of every cloud, however, comes a silver lining, and just before his death he sold his business to Haggards Crowther Accountants, who currently represent me. As an actor's accountant I find them to be all I need. They're perfectly capable of explaining all my affairs to me in layman's terms that I understand.

So, just what do you need to understand as a working actor in terms of accountancy and financial regulation? I spoke to Tim Haggard, one of the partners.

How do I set up my business as an actor?

Having made the big, exciting, nerve-racking decision to go into business as an actor, it's important to get yourself set up to succeed as a business. There are a number of things that you can do immediately:

1. Register as self-employed with HM Revenue & Customs. It's important that you let them know as soon as possible so that you are in the system and paying the appropriate taxes.

2. Speak to the bank and get a separate bank account organised for your business. This is simple and very effective, as it separates your personal affairs from those of your business, and makes the record-keeping straightforward. Take

care to keep your business and personal lives separate by paying for business expenses out of your business account and personal expenses out of your personal account.

3. Find an excellent accountant. A recommendation is most people's preferred route, either from a trusted person in your profession, or from your family. Equity have a list of accountants, and places such as the Actors Centre are often happy to recommend accountants and sometimes offer discounts.

4. Keep receipts for expenses that relate to your work. There are many different types of expenses that may be business-related, and your accountant will be able to tell you what the taxman will allow and those he will not allow. Work-related travel, theatre tickets, Equity subscriptions, and agent's commission are all legitimate expenses. If you have a computer and a working knowledge of Excel, it would be a good idea to list the expenses that you incur as you incur them. Your accountant will provide you with a suitable template.

What taxes do I pay?

The rather fatalistic proverb, 'Nothing is certain in life other than death and taxes', highlights the sad and inevitable difficulty in avoiding the burden of taxes.

The good news is that the taxman gives you a start by not charging income tax on the first £10,000 of earnings.

Class 2 National Insurance contributions start immediately with a payment once every three months. Thereafter you may pay tax and National Insurance in one of two ways:

- *Either*: for a particular job, you will be set up as an employee of the production company. If this is the case, appropriate tax and National Insurance will be deducted by the production company and paid over to HMRC on your behalf.

- *Or*: you are treated as self-employed, in which case you will be asked to submit an invoice, which is paid by the production company without any tax deducted. In this circumstance, the tax will be calculated through your self-assessment tax return.

The practicalities are often arranged by your agent, who will organise the relationship with the production company, receive the money due and then pass the proceeds on to you after deducting their commission.

How does the tax-return process work?

Once you have registered as self-employed, you will be required to file a tax return annually.

Each year, you will need to consolidate all your earnings for the year to 5th April, together with all the allowable expenses, and then the total tax liability due. You will also get a personal allowance that means that the first £10,000 of profit is tax-free. This allowance is changed annually by the government.

HMRC gives you nine months to do this, so the tax return must be filed by the following 31st January.

Whilst you have nine months, I would strongly recommend that you file your return as soon as possible after the 5th April – it provides an early view of the tax due and gives you time to save the money needed to pay the tax bill. You will then need to pay the tax due on 31st January in the following year.

In your second year of trading you will have to pay tax in instalments, called payments on account. Your accountant can advise on this.

How important is it to find the right accountant?

Really important. Your accountant will be a trusted adviser from the start, and whilst he or she will need a fee, a good accountant will save you a lot of time, effort and money. The acting profession has its own set of expenses and case law, so it is also important to find an accountant that understands the specifics of the profession and knows how to apply the general laws to your circumstances; consolidate earnings from various sources and ensure the tax due is correct; claim appropriate expenses on your behalf and identify inefficiencies in the tax system which may have resulted in you overpaying tax.

What can an accountant help me with?

In the early days, your accountant will make sure that you are set up correctly, paying as little tax as possible (within the confines of existing legislation) and that amounts due are paid on time. As your career develops, they should become a trusted adviser to you, as your affairs become more complicated and a wider range of skills are required. PAYE, VAT, personal tax, business tax, year-end accounts, returns – keeping all this up to date is a task that many business owners find difficult or just plain boring. Not everyone's good with figures, so trying to do it yourself could in fact prove much costlier than paying an accountant to do it for you. From a tax perspective, the business is also properly administered, which gives peace of mind and frees you up to do other things. To use a medical analogy, what you should be looking for is a good GP, with links to a specialist if you need one.

What about paying for basic advice?

Your accountant shouldn't charge for occasional basic advice. Anything more than that and you'll probably have to pay, but having to pay for half an hour with your accountant could save you a stack of money.

Do I need an accountant when setting up a business?

You most probably don't for setting up a basic sole-trader business, although you would benefit from paying an accountant to do your returns – some traders do their own, but chasing HMRC can be difficult and time-consuming. Many accountants will even give you free basic start-up advice, if you agree to them doing your accounts. You can set up your own limited company without an accountant, although the bigger, more complex or potentially high-growth the venture, the more advisable it is to seek professional tax advice right from the get-go. You can regret it if you don't.

How do I find an accountant?

Ask actors for recommendations. Equity also have a list of approved accountants for their members. You could do some online research to find good local accountants. For added peace of mind, you could look for members on the websites of such organisations as the ICAEW or ACCA. Shortlist at least four; have a look at their websites; see what they offer. But – crucially – go and see them face to face before deciding. You need to walk away from that meeting confident that they know what they're doing and their services will match your needs and expectations. Always be clear about how much you will have to pay – including any additional fees and charges. Think carefully about whether you want an accountant that is a sole trader (probably at the value end of the market, but can get overwhelmed at busy times if they are doing it all themselves), versus an established local practice with a number of partners and staff (often a good solution as you will get a broad range of technical skills supplied with a personal touch – however, they may be a little expensive if you are starting out), versus a large or national firm (will be more expensive, and focused on their largest clients. You may feel that they have a high turnover of staff – and that it is difficult to get access to partner time). There are a number of online tax services available, but ask the same questions. How much access to specialist advice will you have should the need arise?

How do I get the best out of my relationship with my accountant?

If you value their opinion – act on their advice. Don't bargain them down too hard on price – you may get a deal, but you'll never be top of their priority list. When your accountant asks for something, provide it quickly. If you want to keep the fees down, do what you can to make their job easier.

Any final advice on choosing an accountant?

Only that changing your accountant isn't as hard as you might think – so don't over stress about choosing one. If it isn't working for you, find another accountant – simple as that.

★★★

Tim's advice does rather assume that you have decided you want an accountant. You might be perfectly happy to manage your tax affairs on your own, and that's fine. Equity provide a full list of claimable allowances, and given the fact that we are so frequently told that only 2% of actors earn over £20,000 a year from their acting, you may think an accountant is a little bit of a luxury. The rule of thumb is that the accountant should probably save you more money in tax than they charge you in fees. Remember that their fee is also a tax-deductible expense. I would thoroughly endorse Tim's advice in not haggling, but many accountants do introductory offers. If you do work other than acting as part of your life, then it's important to make sure that you're on the right tax code for that work too. All the income you receive during a year should be declared as part of your tax return, and that's where an accountant can be invaluable. If you've been put on the wrong tax code for a temporary job, and believe me that's not unheard of, then an accountant could be able to claim back tax for you. If you are a low earner, then check out Tax Aid, an absolutely wonderful resource that gives tax advice, and tax-return assistance for those on low incomes.

And, of course, remember to *save* money! Me writing that word is a little like the pot calling the kettle black, but I do know from experience that not saving enough for tax can have disastrous consequences. I once got

£11,000 behind on my tax after a run in the West End, and even though I had agreed a repayment scheme with HMRC, they suddenly decided that they were going to send in the bailiffs. In a coincidence worthy of a Disney movie, on the very day they told me they were taking action, I got a commercial which paid my tax bill and more. I was very lucky. Writing this, I'm hoping that you won't have to rely on luck, but will have the good sense to put money away from every job into a high-interest account to pay your tax. I do now, and I don't regret it.

Work Task

If you don't have one already, open a tax account. You can do it online. It could be a high-interest, limited-access account that will make it harder for you to dip into it on a rainy day.

Get a list of expenses from Equity, keep all your receipts and check that you are claiming everything you can.

Check out accountants, if you don't already have one, and talk to your colleagues and friends in the business about who they use and recommend. I'm sure Tim at Haggards Crowther (www.haggards.co.uk) would be only too pleased to hear from you. Mention that you read about him in this book!

Look at your financial projection for the next year, and work out how many different income sources you will have, both acting and non-acting. The more you have, the more you would benefit from professional assistance and advice.

24. Building your voice reel

There are many occasions when you are not actually acting as an actor and you feel like you'll never work again. Auditions may be thin on the ground, and whatever other work you do may be sparse too. Actors are imaginative and creative creatures, and the mind can begin to wander to other things you might do in order to earn money and to achieve some level of fulfilment and success. In these interconnected information-superhighway days, this sort of lateral thinking can take you to lots of places. In the past, it led to other actor-related skills.

Following up an advertisement in *The Stage*, I made my way right through to studio screen tests as a shopping presenter on QVC. It was not something that I ever really wanted to do, but the advertisement shone out at me one Thursday morning and I applied. After an open audition alongside lots of beautifully made-up models, I turned up at the studio to demonstrate a tabletop juicer, and a switching device that allows you to connect two kitchen appliances to one power supply. In my language I thought it was called a plug, but I seem to remember it had a rather amazing brand name. The practicalities of demonstrating while being spoken to by an increasingly excited producer through an earpiece were nothing compared to the pressures of keeping a straight face. Suddenly, as the cameras rolled, I found myself in the middle of one of the rather more hilarious Victoria Wood sketches, and the ridiculousness of the situation rolled up in my mind like a hysterical fog. I'm pretty sure this must have shown through. They were very courteous about my ability, and asked me to keep in touch, but the best thing about it was that I didn't get the job. It had just been a way of filling my mind, and giving me something to concentrate on for a couple of weeks.

Many actors make very good shopping-channel presenters. Many actors are good at other things and they specialise in those areas. Voice-over, corporate training, presenting; there are actors who make a particular field their speciality. So just dipping a toe into it is hardly likely to make you a success.

If you do want to try and work in the corporate market, you will have to plan your attack. Lots of actors work only in this area and make a great deal of money from it. Similarly, there are actors who just go from voice studio to voice studio, adding their honeyed tones to teabags, tampons, and tempting food commercials, and who are very good at it.

Drama schools sometimes offer a basic training in voice-over technique. Sometimes this is bundled up with the two afternoons during your training when you do radio, but it is a whole industry of its own. Voice work is a speciality. Certainly it's something that you can get into, but you will have to focus your campaign, and spend a lot of time trying to get a foot in the door.

I've been rather lucky in that I have a voice-over agent, but even so I've been called upon to be the voice of

British gravel, the rather hoarse tones of several medical campaigns for local radio, two *Doctor Who* villains (one of whom was a giant slug) and the narrator of a BBC Two docusoap about an aristocratic young gardener and his family trying to hang on to their stately home. All of the jobs were great fun, but I'd hardly call them a career.

If one of your work tasks is improving your chances of employability in the voice-over industry, just what do you have to do? I asked Laura Milne, who runs the voice-over agency The Joneses about what she looks for when actors' voice reels arrive in her inbox.

A good-quality reel, made professionally so that the voice is presented well. The advantage of working with professionals on creating your voice reel is that they can provide you with scripts and material that they may already have in the studio. They will certainly have a good idea of how your voice should sound at its best, and will be able to achieve that quickly. Of course, getting a professional-sounding voice reel made will cost a couple of hundred pounds at the very least. There are lots of reasonably priced recording programmes for both PC and Mac that you can use, but you should ensure you know what you're doing and have good-quality equipment before making something yourself and sending it off to an agent. You don't want their first impression of you to be that you're a bit of an amateur who is playing around.

A unique quality to the voice – a certain gravitas or enunciation, for example. What is the distinctive factor about your voice that you're trying to sell? What is it that makes your voice distinctive from others? It's no good just completing a voice reel where you are impersonating voice-over styles that you have already heard on television. Define the distinction of your voice and ensure that it's clearly demonstrated.

A sense of humour and playfulness. Just as in audition situations where people forget that the perfect audition speech should also be entertaining, sometimes actors are so busy trying to demonstrate their vocal potential, that they forget that the material has to engage. Choose a short but punchy and hopefully funny piece of narrative. A tiny piece of storytelling will allow you to show just what your voice brings to any script.

Contrasting commercials – a straight read, a character read, a campaign read, and a relaxed read, etc. – to show versatility. A fast-paced hard-sell ad perhaps followed by a more leisurely read. A straight read is a good straight narration. Add a viewpoint or an accented tone to that for a character read. A campaign read is a fast, punchy, informative piece, and a relaxed read is probably your true self telling someone a story. And actually all of those could be contained in a well-edited ninety-second reel. Remember, if your reel is emailed out to potential voice agents, nobody is going to spend a lot of time listening to five minutes of material. If they're not interested within the first twenty seconds, then they probably won't listen to the rest of it.

Commercials in the natural voice. Sometimes people think that a voice reel should really be an accent and dialect taster. Stick to your strength. If there is an accent that you are particularly known for on television, other than your native accent, then this can be added, but only one.

Creativity and confidence in your delivery. You need to ensure that you believe in the commercial. This is when the magic happens. Try and think what the original brief for that commercial must have been for that actor, rather than thinking you can use the script of a commercial to demonstrate something else. Work with the writing, not against it. Find the material that allows your creativity to breathe.

***

The best book I've read on the subject of voice work is called *The VoiceOver Book: Don't Eat Toast* by Stephen Kemble and David Hodge. It's a brilliantly informed and instructional guide to the whole industry, from people who really know what they're talking about.

Finding your voice is not something that may come easily, but it's something worth investing a little time in. Even if your conclusion is that the voice-over market is not something you want to go into, at least it means that your energies will be diverted into more productive channels. And who knows? When you make it big, you will be writing a biography. And then you can record the audiobook!

Work Task

Using a voice recorder or your phone, or your computer, read several styles and listen to them back. Read a news item, a commercial, and an extract from a novel. Try to define what it is that makes your voice different. Accent? Tone? Timbre?

If you are computer literate, make a small test reel using something like GarageBand or Audacity. Get feedback from actors you know who do voice-overs, or perhaps from your agent.

25. Taping yourself

As we have well and truly entered the digital world, so the demands made upon us as actors have changed. Everything moves at a much quicker pace these days. Castings happen with very little notice. When I started out, my agent would call with news of a casting two or three days in advance. Nowadays they nearly always ring with something for the next day. This means that, as actors, we have to be more adaptable and ready to move quickly. At many castings these days you are very lucky to meet even the casting director, as often the first round of auditions for any television-drama project are conducted by a casting assistant – the main objective of the session being just to 'put you on tape'. From these initial meetings, a selection will be made of people who may come in and read with the director at a later date. It's no wonder, then, that the American fashion for self-taping is creeping into our world.

All the major casting services are acknowledging that self-taping is here to stay. Spotlight has a state-of-the-art self-tape studio with cameraman and editor – top quality, but expensive. The Actors Centre has a do-it-yourself tape facility with lights, microphones and backdrops, at £20 for half an hour. Casting Networks also have a facility for you to upload an audition for a casting director to see. There are many advantages. The casting director can get a lot of people reading the scene very quickly, and can make sure that the people the director actually meets are in line with the way they want the role played. It allows them to hear you actually speaking the dialogue and to begin to see the decisions you would make when playing the role. For the actor, self-taping can save you money. Even if you're London-based, it can cost the best part of £15 to get into and out of Central London for a quick ten-minute audition. The facility to be able to tape that audition in the comfort of your own home, recording and re-recording until you are happy with it, and then submit it online, allows you to manage your free time more effectively.

But let's be honest. If the phone rang now and your agent asked you to submit a self-taped audition within the next two hours, could you actually do it? Remember, this is going to be something that has to show you in a good light, look professional, and hopefully get you into the casting room. So what do you need to make a good self-taped audition, and how should you go about it?

Most people have the basic equipment to hand in the form of a smartphone. Whether it's Android or iOS, any smartphone that has the facility to record video will do. If you're still being so last century and don't have a phone with this facility, then a digital video camera that can upload footage to a laptop or computer will also do. You can also use webcams built into a laptop or computer, but these are rather limited as to where you can shoot. The great thing about a smartphone is that you can record on the go. A friend of mine recently received a call from his agent asking for a self-taped scene to be sent back within two hours while he was in a hotel in Swansea filming a drama series. All the other actors were out on location, but with the help of a barman with thespian leanings, and a good knowledge of what he could do on his phone, he managed to get a pretty decent audition uploaded and sent back to London within sixty minutes.

So you just received a script from your agent. They want a taped audition of it within a couple of hours. The first thing to do is just as you would for any audition – learn the scene. Spend time thinking about the decisions you're going to make for the character, and focus on the piece. When you have learned the scene, then move on to self-taping.

Ideally you will have a stand for your smartphone, or you may even invest in a holder which allows you to place the phone on a small tripod. Someone could hold the phone for you, and they might be able to oblige by reading in lines. Check the frame. A good framing is a medium close-up of your head and shoulders. The top of the frame should be above your head without much space in between. A nice straight-on angle is best, and ideally shot against a plain background. A pale blue or pale green background are most effective and push the face forward, but any plain wall without distractions will be good. Think about where in your home you could shoot this.

The brightest object in the shot should be your face, so pay some attention to lighting. It may well be that you can shoot in natural light, which will be all well and good. Try to eliminate any shadows. You don't need to be a lighting expert, but just look around the home and see if you have a desk lamp, or a light that can be used to lift the background. A basic lighting configuration would be one strong light on one side balanced by a smaller diffused light on the opposite side. A diffused light is one that is reflected onto the subject, or filtered through a lighting shade. Experimentation is fine, but don't try and get arty. Make sure your face is lit and can be seen clearly.

Think about what you might wear in just the same way that you would if you were attending an audition. You wouldn't go in full costume, but you would wear something appropriate. Self-taping isn't an excuse to raid the dressing-up box, but a little thought about what you are wearing will help the overall effect. Don't wear loud patterns. Colours that fade into the background may give an odd effect. We've all seen headshots with people in black shirts against black backgrounds, and this can give a 'floating head' effect. A self-taped audition, after all, is a talking headshot. It's about you, it's not about your wardrobe. If in doubt, neutral and plain.

You've probably been sent a scene to read and an ideal solution is to get somebody to read in with you from behind the camera, preferably a friend who is an actor, or someone you trust and who knows what they are doing. Get them to sit where your eyeline will be, which should be close to the camera and to the left or right of it. Do you know which is your strongest pro-file? It certainly might be beneficial to record the scene twice with an eyeline to both sides of camera and then make a final call upon which you think looks best. Unless you have been specifically asked to, do not record the piece looking direct to camera. Similarly, it can be distracting if you give an ident to camera, i.e. saying your name and agent to camera, and then turn-ing and beginning the scene. If your video-editing knowledge is good enough, it may be best to caption the final clip with your name and agent, so that during the piece you stay within scene. Shoot a test clip first to check that you are happy with how everything looks and sounds.

If time allows, there is no reason that you shouldn't record multiple takes. Try different readings and different approaches, but ultimately you will have to choose just one to send into the casting director, or to your agent. For this reason, you should keep the shoot simple. One shot, well framed and close, will tell the story. At the very most, and only if you have someone operating the camera who knows what they are doing, you could start the shot a little wider and tighten in as the scene continues to bring the focus in to yourself, but if you're not sure how to do this, then don't do it.

If you do use iOS there is a fantastic app called Videon (premium app £2.99 from the App Store), which allows you to shoot and edit the footage on your phone. Otherwise you can transfer the footage onto a computer and use Windows Movie Maker, iMovie, QuickTime, or any video-editing software. Don't get carried away by all the transitions and cuts the software can do. Keep it simple.

Save the clip in the best resolution and highest quality that you can, and then send it to your agent or to the casting director. If you've been given any instructions from the casting director as to how they would like to receive the clip, then follow them to the letter. They may have asked that the file size is limited to a certain number of megabytes. If your file is bigger than that, it may be rejected by their server. Check the file size and, if necessary, use your video-editing software to reduce it to something that is easily emailable. On a Mac these days you can send file sizes up to several gigabytes. With Windows it's slightly different, but you can always use a file-transfer site such as Dropbox, WeTransfer, or Hightail. With these services you upload the file from your computer, and the recipient is sent a link to the site where they can download the file. Ask them to acknowledge receipt of the file so that you know your hard work has actually reached its destination.

Work Task

Make a self-tape of a new audition speech. Work out where in your home you have a good background, and download any apps or programmes you need to complete the task. Don't wait until your agent actually rings and asks you to self-tape, make sure that you have the process working for you so that when the call does come, you can concentrate on the scene rather than the process.

26. Being a Working Actor

Now you have lots of creative ideas that will help you as a Working Actor: things to do that will move your business forward, even though you may not actually be doing any acting right now. Good businesses need a business plan and that's no different for you. A map of things you want to achieve during the coming months or so. A Plan. A great way forward and making the most of the ideas you now have. You should decide how long this plan is for. Is it going to be for the next year? Is it just to be for the next few months? There's an awful lot to be said for taking an afternoon and making a plan for the coming year: actually physically creating a document which becomes a work plan. A good work plan will have objectives, tasks, and results. Putting these together in one place can be a useful focusing exercise. It will allow you to move forward knowing exactly what you're aiming for. It should also help you focus on the steps you need to make it work.

Think of what we have talked about earlier. SMART objectives. Specific, Measurable, Attainable, Relevant, Timed. Timed should be easy. If you're making this plan for a year, then your target for completion of all these objectives is one year hence, preferably one calendar year from the day you're making the plan. Set yourself a series of objectives that cover all aspects of your Working Actor life. Financial, skills and jobs. The more objectives you have achieved by the end of the year, the more successful you will feel, and the more resilient, engaged and motivated you will be for the next year. You might want to use a spreadsheet, or just make a list in a notebook. Buy one specifically for the purpose, and use it to collect your thoughts and experiences. If your work objectives meet the SMART criteria, then you don't need to make a huge long list of them. Someone who lists ten objectives for the next year and only meets two of them could barely be said to be successful. Someone who makes five specific and relevant objectives and finds that, in one year's time, he or she has met four of them will have a greater feeling of achievement.

We all need dreams, but dreams are not objectives. Is it realistic, or attainable, to set yourself an objective in all fields, i.e. television, theatre, and film? That may be your criteria. Perhaps you might aim to have two days' paid work on a nationally transmitted piece of television, one short student film and six nights on stage over the next twelve months. All probably attainable with or without the help of an agent, and a target that certainly helps you to focus when looking for work. You may already have several television credits, and therefore want to make your objective a little more specific. You may want to categorise it: work on a soap opera, work on a piece of children's television, work on a drama. Don't limit yourself too much, but be as specific as you can. *Midsomer Murders* has been on my objectives for about ten years and I'm still working at it. Having done that, and if you have an agent, this would be a good excuse to sit down and have that conversation with them about what you're looking for, and how you are looking to move forward during the next year. They won't be able to promise that they will be able to do something about it, but it's good that they know – and it's good that they know you are thinking in those terms.

To make sure that the 'Working Actor' ethos works fully, you will also have to set yourself financial objectives for the year. This can be daunting, but is well worth doing. It can help you work out just when you can look at the prospective of low-paid work for productivity and exposure, and when your primary need is just to earn. Two months and £5,000 away from your target date would seem to suggest that money then becomes a priority. Start with living expenses. Total them for the year. Add Spotlight or whichever casting service you are going to subscribe to. Add Equity membership, if you feel it is of value to you. Work out travel – monthly, weekly or daily. Allow yourself money for headshots, classes or workshops as you think fit. Total these and you have an idea of what your basic financial objective will need to be. All the money you earn, whether from acting, subsidiary jobs using your acting skills, benefits due to you, or just other jobs helping you to pay your way, will count towards this target. You can divide the total sum by twelve to give you a monthly budget objective, which can make it easier to see where you are as the year progresses. Writing down these figures can be depressing, but it really can help to make the picture clearer. It also gives you twelve milestones during the year where you see just how you're doing. You may end up doing lots of promotional work, or spending a great deal of time serving behind a bar, but if you have the evidence on paper that it is helping you meet your objectives, it is helping you on your way to success.

In business terms, it's considered most effective to set yourself five objectives. A manager reviewing someone's work at the end of the year would consider them to be on track if they have completed three of those fully, and done reasonably well on the other two. Take a moment to think how you might come up with five objectives.

Here are some examples:

1. Number of days worked as an actor during the year.

2. Income throughout the year. (Acting and non-acting income combined – or separate? Your choice.)

3. Four days on set in front of a camera – at least one day to be on a programme that is transmitted on national television.

4. Five nights appearing on stage, paid or unpaid.

5. Five days' work in corporate or promotional.

6. To get at least eight auditions throughout the year.

7. To get a new showreel/voice reel.

8. To join the Actors Centre.

9. To read four playscripts or four acting books.

Now, I would have thought that's a reasonably achievable set of targets, unless, of course, you enter the figure £75,000 in objective two! To be able to look back at the end of the year and have achieved three of those objectives would mean that you were in no bad state in terms of regularity of work, or income. The financial objective can tend to overrule some of the others, in that finding money to live on is absolutely key.

Having set the objectives, the next part of the plan is to work out what you will do to achieve them. Each objective should have four or five tasks listed below it in the manner of the work tasks that I have listed throughout this book. That means that, instantly, from the day after you create this list, you have at least twenty tasks to set out and achieve. After the tasks you have created that you think will lead you to your objectives, look through the list starting on page 243 which is a summary of all the work tasks that have been covered at the end of the various chapters in this book. Choose the ones that you feel apply to you. List them in order of importance and add them to the list of tasks that you have created from your objectives. You now probably have somewhere in the region of forty or fifty items on your Working Actor list. At the rate of achieving five every working week, that's eight to ten weeks of tasks, and an awful lot can happen in that time. There is space at the end of the list printed here for you to add your own tasks.

Don't wait until your task list is finished before making another. The huge injection of energy that will be needed when you have completed a list of forty tasks to create another one can be an enormous obstacle. Make this an ongoing process.

You can add a new task every day, or you can add a series of tasks to your list at the end of each week. Some of these may be repeat tasks – checking theatre websites for casting information, checking the casting services job pages, Equity job service, and various web-sites for short-film information. Some will be new tasks created from information that you have gained. Vary the tasks. A week of letter-writing will be exceptionally dull and, if you receive no replies, will also feel very pointless. One day to send letters or emails, one day looking at a new skill or practising something at home, such as self-taping or sight-reading. One day meeting someone to discuss what is out there – a friend, an agent or a work colleague. Vary what you demand of yourself. It helps to keep the ongoing business of being a Working Actor fresh.

In life, as in the dramas we want to be acting in, things will happen that are totally unexpected. You can't plan for that phone call from your agent which will give you the audition you never thought possible, but if that's all you're waiting for, it will never come. The kettle of ambition never boils while it's being watched. When you're getting on with things and you have turned your attention away from waiting to *doing*, that's when things happen. The joy of your life as a Working Actor is that on any day something unexpected could happen that will change your life for ever. But just sitting around waiting for that is no way to live a life. You are an actor. You wanted to be an actor. You have worked hard to be an actor. You have made a considerable out-lay financially or emotionally, and often both, to do this. So do it. Do it with style. Do it wholeheartedly. Do it every day. Be a Working Actor.

Work Task List

Here is a short summary of the work tasks listed throughout the book. This can be a key part of your Working Actor plan.

✓ Write down five things that differentiate you from any other actor.

✓ Looking through the *Radio Times* or online listings, make a list of all the production companies that produce the sort of drama or comedy you feel you would like to be cast in.

✓ Make a list of all the theatres that you would like to work at: not only major companies, but find five fringe venues in which you'd also like to appear. Check out the casting requirements in the forthcoming programmes for all the theatres you've listed. Highlight the roles for which you would be suitable and then find the casting deadlines for those productions.

✓ Check the Equity job information service and set a diary reminder to do it regularly.

✓ Try out a free profile on various casting services, such as CastNet and Casting Networks.

✓ Log into Spotlight and make sure your casting filters define the roles that are sent to you. Update your CV and check that your photographs and showreel are up to date. Look through the podcasts and articles available to you as a Spotlight member. Download one podcast to listen to tomorrow.

✓ Make a list of the top-ten film courses and email them to find out who is head of the course and responsible for casting student films.

✓ Check out the websites such as www.shootingpeople.org and www.mandy.com, where student and short-film requirements are often advertised.

✓ Check that your domain name is available to buy and register it. Try out a free website production service and build a trial web page.

✓ Select three people you're going to write a letter to in the next five days. Plan and write the letter.

✓ As part of your Working Actor plan, set five objectives that fit the SMART criteria.

✓ Try and sit on the other side of an audition desk.

✓ Prep your next meeting.

✓ Find and learn a new audition speech that is also entertaining.

✓ Check out NLP for Actors and try out some of their exercises.

✓ Check out the Equity website and have a look at the articles and information that is available for you as a member, or join if you haven't as yet.

✓ Write down a list of what you feel your agent does for you and what you feel your agent should do. Have a face-to-face meeting to chat it through.

✓ Research and plan your new headshot.

✓ Make yourself a casting checklist.

✓ Download the free version of some acting apps and give them a try.

✓ Check out role-play companies, promotional companies, and call centres who use actors, and examine what the work opportunities are for between jobs.

✓ Take a look at the Actors Centre, and The Actors' Guild and The So & So Arts Club. Have a look at their workshop programmes and book yourself a workshop.

✓ Give yourself a full check on all the benefits that you are claiming for. Make an appointment for advice (free if a member) at Equity if you are not sure.

✓ Review your social media. Take a look at your Facebook settings, and your Twitter settings. If you don't have an account on either, could an account on one of these actually help promote your work?

✓ Open a tax account to save money for tax. Get a list of expenses from Equity and check out accountants.

✓ Make yourself a trial voice reel. Get some feedback on it and think about investing in a professional voice reel.

✓ Self-tape an audition speech you have learned.

✓ Make your Working Actor plan.

Also by Paul Clayton

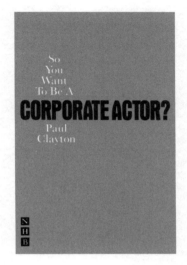

So You Want To Be A **CORPORATE ACTOR?** Paul Clayton

The first book published about the increasingly accessible and lucrative business of corporate acting – training, role-plays, Forum Theatre and live events.

'**For actors wishing to utilise their theatrical skills within the corporate world, this book should be their bible. It is crystal clear, informative and irreverent – and lays out in simple terms how actors need to think and present themselves to be employable.**' *Janet Rawson, Co-founder of Steps Drama Learning Development*

Get 25% off this and all Nick Hern Books titles
Just use code WORKINGACTOR at
www.nickhernbooks.co.uk

Other Essential Books for Actors
from Nick Hern Books

Get 25% off all Nick Hern Books titles
Just use code WORKINGACTOR at
www.nickhernbooks.co.uk

www.nickhernbooks.co.uk

 facebook.com/nickhernbooks

twitter.com/nickhernbooks